Pocket Guide
to
Depression Glass

Revised Eighth Edition

Gene Florence

COLLECTOR BOOKS
A Division of Schroeder Publishing Co., Inc.

Notice

The current values in this book should be used only as a guide. They are not intended to set prices, which vary from one section of the country to another. Auction prices as well as dealer prices vary greatly and are affected by condition as well as demand. Neither the Author nor the Publisher assumes responsibility for any losses that might be incurred as a result of consulting this guide.

A listing of the colors to be found in each pattern is mentioned under the photo headings. However, the prices catalogued herein represent those colors most commonly collected in each pattern. See *The Collector's Encyclopedia of Depression Glass* should you desire more detailed information.

Searching For A Publisher?

We are always looking for knowledgeable people considered to be experts within their fields. If you feel that there is a real need for a book on your collectible subject and have a large comprehensive collection, contact us.

COLLECTOR BOOKS
P.O. Box 3009
Paducah, Kentucky 42002–3009

Foreword

Depression Glass as defined in this book is the colored glassware made primarily during the Depression years in the colors of amber, green, pink, blue, red, yellow, white and crystal. There are other colors and some of the glassware included in this book was made later than the Depression era; but it has still been collected as that era glassware because of its color. The main emphasis of this book is given to the inexpensively made glassware produced in quantity and sold through the five and dime stores or given away as premiums or included with the purchase of other products, i.e. the spice shaker contained in a certain brand spice.

Information of this book has come from over 1,500,000 miles of travel throughout the country in connection with glassware over the past 22 years and from the research and sale of over 600,000 copies of *The Collector's Encyclopedia of Depression Glass*.

Acknowledgments

I would like at this time to say a word of thanks to the people who generously lent their glassware to be photographed. They are as follows: Lois Florence, my sister, and my mother, Gladys Florence, of Grannie Bear Antiques.

Also, a special thanks to my family for their support in various ways, gathering bits of information, taking over my responsibilities to leave me free to write.

A special thanks to Tom Clouser, Curtis and Mays Photographic Studio & Gallery of Paducah, Kentucky, for the photographs in the book.

I wish to thank Lisa Stroup and Jane White of Collector Books for their work in photographing and putting this book together.

Pricing

Glass that is in less than mint condition, i.e. chipped, cracked, scratched or poorly molded, will bring very small prices unless extremely rare, and then, will bring only a small percentage of the price of glass that is in mint condition.

This book is meant as a guide to price; however, if your Depression Glass comes to you at bargain rates or free from a relative, then that's all to the good!

Prices have become almost standarized due to national advertising by dealers and due to the Depression Glass shows which are held from coast to coast. However, there are some regional differences in prices due to glass being more readily available in some areas of the country than in others. Too, companies distributed certain pieces in some areas that it did not in others.

Contents

How To Find Depression Glass

The best place to find Depression Glass is in your own basement, garage or attic – or even in your own cupboards. Yes, that's true. Nearly everyone has at least a piece or two around their own home; it may be a bowl that belonged to grandmother and got handed down; it may be a complete setting that an aunt or someone got as a wedding gift and packed away for storage in the attic.

First of all, you need to learn to recognize the colors of Depression Glass, for often the coloring of the glass is recognizable as Depression era glassware even when the pattern name is yet unknown. That was primarily the reason for making this book a full-color book so that the novice collector could acquaint himself with the full range of colors the glass may be found in.

Once you have searched your own shelves and those of your immediate relatives and friends, your next source for finding Depression Glass should be the garage sales, tag sales, yard sales, etc. where people are cleaning out their attics and garages. Don't forget the church bazaar, the Salvation Army store or the Volunteers of America. You'll find competition is keen at these latter places, so you'll need to shop early.

Now that you've covered all the aforementioned places, it's time to make a tour of the antique and junk shops in your area. These are often gold mines of the ridiculous to the sublime price-wise, so have in mind what you'll pay for a particular item. Too, most of these shops expect to haggle a bit over price, so don't be shy.

Household and estate auctions are often another valuable source for finding Depression Glass, but it is wise to check out the merchandise before making a bid as chips and small damage to an item may be overlooked by the harried auctioneer.

Many collectors feel that antique shows and flea markets are the very best places to find Depression Glass. So, don't forget to put these on your agenda.

I find my best sources for finding the particular pieces and patterns in Depression Glass are the Depression Glass shows held by clubs throughout the country and a publication which deals primarily in Depression era glass. You will find a listing on page 159 of this book. There are other publications, of course, but for overall information and volume of advertisement of glass, the *Daze* is it.

Selling

One of the purposes of this book is to help you make money from any of your unwanted glassware treasures. Any number of books imply that there are treasures in your attic, but few tell you how to reap benefits from them. To find a reputable dealer in your area is not always an easy task, but here are a few suggestions. If you live in an area where a show is held regularly, watch for advertisements and attend the show. You might find a buyer for your glass among the dealers at the show. If there is a Depression Glass Club meeting in your area, there may be members there who would be willing to buy your glass or who could put you in contact with someone who would. Failing either of those methods, you could send for a sample copy of one of the publications listed at the end of the book and seek a dealer in your area by looking through the ads. The telephone directory or the ads under "Antiques" in you local newspaper may lead you to a dealer in glass who would be interested in buying yours; or you might take it to a local flea market and find a buyer among the dealers set up there.

The prices herein are retail and you can expect to receive 50 to 70% of the prices listed for the popular, highly collectible patterns, but only 35 to 50% of prices listed for the patterns that are not as avidly sought by collectors.

There are several factors a dealer will consider when offering for your piece: its condition, how popular this color is with potential buyers, whether or not the pattern is one numerous people collect, whether he has plenty in stock already, or whether he thinks he can make money on the piece before he's had to pack it up at 65 different shows throughout the country and dropped it and broken it. Popularity of a pattern and the demand for it are the two key factors in interesting a potential buyer of your glassware. This book should give you an accurate guide as to what to expect for your glass. You shouldn't be walking up to a dealer without the faintest idea of what your glass is worth; neither should you expect him to pay you retail price for the glass if you're sincerely wanting him to buy it.

What To Collect
Helpful Hint Section

Many beginning collectors make the mistake of trying to collect everything in sight. Unless you have a few oil wells on the side, you can soon find yourself out of funds doing this.

My first suggestion is to study this book. Most of you have looked at the pictures before even starting to read this; that's a start. You have a general idea of what's available. Decide on one or possibly two patterns you like. Once you see it close at hand, you may change your mind; but that's all right. Collectors do that for a variety of reasons. However, it's wise to settle on something specific to look for rather than to pick and choose at random.

If money is a problem, peruse the prices of the various patterns and choose one that is less expensive to collect. However, you should become familiar with the whole range of patterns and you should have a general idea of the range of prices on the more expensive pieces of the patterns because everyone, sooner or later, stumbles onto a piece of glass worth $50.00 that's priced at $5.00. Even if you don't care for the piece or the pattern, you should go ahead and buy it because you'll either be able to trade it to someone who does want it for the pattern you want, or you can sell it and use the extra money to buy the glass you like.

In the early 1960's through the early 1970's, you could buy Depression Glass by the box and crate loads at auctions for a song; thus, you could afford to collect several patterns at once. However, those days have come to an end; so it's better to have something definite in mind to collect.

If money is no problem, then by all means, choose one of the more expensive patterns to collect. Since there are more people wanting these patterns usually, the market value of your pattern will be stable at the least, and will probably increase as the years pass.

Some people don't choose to collect an entire pattern. They collect one piece of every pattern, maybe plates for example. One California collector collects only cookie jars; another I know collects only candy jars; and there are numerous salt and pepper collections. So you could choose to collect only one or two pieces of several patterns. In any case, you'll find the glass attractive to serve in and a real item of conversation.

If you are hard-bitten by the bug of collecting Depression Glass, then you might possibly want a more detailed guide for the glass. Should that happen, I'd be delighted to recommend my *Collector's Encyclopedia of Depression Glass,* which can be ordered from this publisher or myself. I receive letters daily from its delighted readers. In any case, happy hunting – and even happier finding. It's a hobby I think you'll not only enjoy but one from which you'll profit.

ADAM
(See Reproduction Section, Page 137)
(pink, green, crystal, yellow, delphite)
JEANNETTE GLASS COMPANY, 1932–1934

	Pink	Green
Ashtray, 4½"	25.00	20.00
Bowl, 4¾" Dessert	13.50	13.50
Bowl, 5¾" Cereal	35.00	35.00
Bowl, 7¾"	18.00	20.00
Bowl, 9" Covered	50.00	80.00
Bowl, 10" Oval	22.50	23.00
Butter Dish & Cover	70.00	275.00
Cake Plate, 10" Footed	20.00	23.00
Candlesticks, 4", Pr.	75.00	85.00
Candy Jar & Cover, 2½"	70.00	87.50
Coaster, 3¾"	18.00	16.00
Creamer	16.00	18.00
Cup	21.00	19.00
Lamp	235.00	260.00
Pitcher, 8", 32 oz.	35.00	40.00

	Pink	Green
Plate, 6" Sherbet	7.00	7.50
Plate, 7¾" Sq. Salad	10.00	11.00
Plate, 9" Sq. Dinner	22.50	20.00
Plate, 9" Grill	16.00	15.00
Platter, 11¾"	17.50	18.00
Relish Dish, 8" Divided	16.00	20.00
Salt & Pepper, 4"	60.00	90.00
Saucer, Sq. 6"	6.50	6.50
Sherbet, 3"	25.00	35.00
Sugar	15.00	17.00
Sugar/Candy Cover	20.00	35.00
Tumbler, 4½"	25.00	22.50
Tumbler, 5½" Iced Tea	50.00	40.00
Vase, 7½"	225.00	45.00

AMERICAN PIONEER
(pink, green, amber, crystal)
LIBERTY WORKS, 1931–1934

	Pink	Green
Bowl, 5" Handled	14.00	16.00
Bowl, 8¾" Covered	85.00	110.00
Bowl, 9" Handled	17.50	22.50
Bowl, Console, 10⅜"	47.50	57.50
Candlesticks, 6½", Pr.	60.00	80.00
Candy Jar & Cover, 1 lb.	75.00	90.00
Candy Jar & Cover, 1½ lb.	80.00	110.00
Cheese & Cracker Set (indented platter & compote)	45.00	55.00
Coaster, 3½"	25.00	27.50
Creamer, 2¾"	17.50	19.50
Creamer, 3½"	18.00	20.00
Cup	9.00	11.00
Dresser Set (2 colognes, Powder jar, on indented 7½" tray)	325.00	295.00
Goblet, Wine, 4", 3 oz.	33.00	45.00
Goblet, Water, 6", 8 oz.	35.00	40.00
Ice Bucket, 6"	40.00	50.00

	Pink	Green
Lamp, 8½" Tall	80.00	97.50
Mayonnaise, 4¼"	55.00	85.00
Pitcher, 5" Covered Urn	125.00	195.00
Pitcher, 7" Covered Urn	145.00	200.00
Plate, 6"	12.00	14.00
Plate, 6" Handled	12.00	15.00
Plate, 8"	7.50	10.00
Plate, 11½" Handled	15.00	16.00
Saucer	4.50	6.00
Sherbet, 3½"	15.00	17.00
Sherbet, 4¾"	24.00	32.00
Sugar, 2¾"	17.50	19.50
Sugar, 3½"	17.50	20.00
Tumbler, 5 oz. Juice	24.00	30.00
Tumbler, 4", 8 oz.	24.00	44.00
Tumbler, 5", 12 oz.	35.00	45.00
Vase, 7", three styles, rolled or crimped edge, straight	70.00	90.00
Whiskey, 2¼", 2 oz.	40.00	

AMERICAN SWEETHEART
(pink, monax, cremax, red and blue)
MacBETH-EVANS GLASS COMPANY, 1930–1936

	Pink	Monax		Pink	Monax
Bowl, 3¾" Flat, Berry	32.50	----	Plate, 15½"	----	175.00
Bowl, 4½" Cream Soup	65.00	95.00	Platter, 13" Oval..............	40.00	55.00
Bowl, 6" Cereal	12.50	10.00	Pitcher, 7½", 60 oz.	500.00	----
Bowl, 9" Round, Berry	35.00	50.00	Pitcher, 8", 80 oz.	425.00	----
Bowl, 9½" Flat Soup	50.00	65.00	Salt & Pepper, Footed ...	250.00	275.00
Bowl, 11" Oval Vegetable ..	50.00	60.00	Saucer	4.00	3.00
Bowl, 18" Console	----	350.00	Sherbet, Footed, 3¾"......	15.00	----
Creamer, Footed	10.00	9.00	Sherbet, Footed, 4¼"	12.00	15.00
Cup	14.00	9.00	Sugar, Open, Footed	9.50	7.00
Plate, 6" Bread & Butter ..	4.50	4.00	Sugar Cover	----	185.00
Plate, 8" Salad	9.50	8.00	Tumbler, 3½", 5 oz	65.00	----
Plate, 9" Luncheon	----	9.00	Tumbler, 4¼", 9 oz.	60.00	----
Plate, 9¾"-10¼" Dinner	30.00	20.00	Tumbler, 4¾", 10 oz.	85.00	----
Plate, 12" Salver	14.00	15.00			

ANNIVERSARY
(pink) (recently in crystal and iridescent)
JEANNETTE GLASS COMPANY, 1947–1949

	Crystal	Pink		Crystal	Pink
Bowl, 4⅞" Berry	3.00	6.00	Plate, 9" Dinner	5.00	9.00
Bowl, 7⅜" Soup	6.50	14.00	Plate, 12½" Sandwich		
Bowl, 9" Fruit	9.00	20.00	Server	5.00	10.00
Butter Dish & Cover	25.00	50.00	Relish Dish, 8"	5.00	9.00
Candy Jar & Cover	17.50	37.50	Saucer	1.50	2.00
Compote, Open, 3 Legged	4.00	10.00	Sherbet, Footed	3.00	7.00
Cake Plate, 12½"	6.50	14.00	Sugar	2.50	7.00
Cake Plate with Cover	14.00	15.00	Sugar Cover	5.00	9.00
Creamer, Footed	4.00	8.50	Vase, 6½"	12.00	25.00
Cup	3.50	6.50	Vase, Wall Pin-up	13.50	25.00
Pickle Dish, 9"	4.00	10.00	Wine Glass, 2½ oz.	7.00	15.00
Plate, 6¼" Sherbet	1.50	2.50			

AUNT POLLY
(green, blue, iridescent)
U.S. GLASS COMPANY, Late 1920s

	Green	Blue		Green	Blue
Bowl, 4⅜" Berry	7.50	13.00	Pitcher, 8", 48 oz.	----	155.00
Bowl, 4¾", 2" High	9.50	18.00	Plate, 6" Sherbet	5.00	11.00
Bowl, 7¼" Oval, Handled Pickle	10.00	35.00	Plate, 8" Luncheon	----	17.50
Bowl, 7⅞" Large Berry	17.00	37.50	Salt & Pepper	----	195.00
Bowl, 8⅜" Oval	35.00	80.00	Sherbet	8.00	11.00
Butter Dish & Cover	210.00	180.00	Sugar	22.50	30.00
Candy, Cover, Two Handled	57.50	----	Sugar Cover	45.00	125.00
Creamer	25.00	40.00	Tumbler, 3⅝", 8 oz.	----	25.00
			Vase, 6½", Footed	27.50	40.00

AURORA
(cobalt)
HAZEL ATLAS COMPANY, 1937–1938

	Cobalt		Cobalt
Bowl, 4½"	27.50	Plate, 6½"	10.00
Bowl, 5⅜"	14.00	Saucer	5.00
Creamer, 4½"	17.50	Tumbler, 4¾"	17.50
Cup	10.00		

AVOCADO, "SWEET PEAR," No. 601
(See Reproduction Section, Page 138)
(pink, green)
INDIANA GLASS COMPANY, 1923–1933

	Pink	Green		Pink	Green
Bowl, 5¼", Two-Handled ...	24.00	28.00	Pitcher, 64 oz.	625.00	795.00
Bowl, 6" Relish, Footed ..	22.50	24.00	Plate, 6¾" Sherbet	13.00	15.00
Bowl, 7" Preserve, One			Plate, 8¼" Luncheon	16.00	18.00
Handle	17.50	24.00	Plate, 10¼" Two Handled		
Bowl, 7½" Salad	30.00	47.50	Cake............................	32.00	47.50
Bowl, 8" Oval,			Saucer	24.00	26.00
Two-Handled	18.50	25.00	Sherbet............................	47.50	52.00
Bowl, 9½", 3¼" Deep	85.00	110.00	Sugar, Footed	30.00	32.00
Creamer, Footed	30.00	32.00	Tumbler	130.00	195.00
Cup, Footed, ...	28.00	30.00			

BEADED BLOCK

(pink, green, crystal, ice blue, vaseline, iridescent, amber, opalescent colors)
IMPERIAL GLASS COMPANY, 1927–1930s

	Green	Opalescent		Green	Opalescent
Bowl, 4½", Two-Handled Jelly	7.00	16.00	Bowl, 7½", Round Fluted Edges	18.00	25.00
Bowl, 4½", Round, Lily	9.00	18.00	Bowl, 7½", Round, Plain Edge	17.50	20.00
Bowl, 5½", Square	7.00	10.00	Bowl, 8¼", Celery	12.50	18.00
Bowl, 5½", One Handle	7.00	12.00	Creamer	15.00	27.50
Bowl, 6", Deep, Round	10.00	18.00	Pitcher, 5¼", Pint Jug	95.00	----
Bowl, 6¼", Round	7.50	16.00	Plate, 7¾" Square	6.50	10.00
Bowl, 6½", Round	7.50	16.00	Plate, 8¾", Round	15.00	19.00
Bowl, 6½", Two-Handled Pickle	12.00	18.00	Stemmed Jelly, 4½"	9.00	18.00
Bowl, 6¾", Round, Unflared	11.00	16.00	Stemmed Jelly, 4½", Flared Top	10.00	18.00
Bowl, 7¼", Round, Flared	12.00	17.50	Sugar	14.00	24.00
			Vase, 6", Bouquet	12.00	22.50

BLOCK OPTIC, "BLOCK"
(green, yellow, pink, crystal)
HOCKING GLASS COMPANY, 1929–1933

	Pink	Green		Pink	Green
Bowl, 4¼", Berry	6.50	7.00	Plate, 8", Luncheon	4.00	5.00
Bowl, 5¼", Cereal	20.00	11.00	Plate, 9", Dinner	25.00	17.50
Bowl, 7¼", Salad	----	20.00	Salt & Pepper, Footed	70.00	35.00
Bowl, 8½", Large Berry	20.00	24.00	Salt & Pepper, Squatty	----	75.00
Butter Dish & Cover, 3"x5"	----	45.00	Sandwich Server, Center		
Candlesticks, 1¾", Pr.	70.00	95.00	Handle	45.00	50.00
Candy Jar & Cover,			Saucer, 2 Sizes, Cup Ring	7.00	9.00
2¼" Tall	45.00	42.50	Sherbet, Non-Stemmed		
Candy Jar Cover, 6¼" Tall	95.00	45.00	(Cone)	----	4.00
Compote, 4" Wide			Sherbet, 3¼", 5½ oz.	7.00	5.00
Mayonnaise	60.00	26.00	Sherbet, 4¾", 6 oz.	14.00	14.00
Creamer, Three Styles:			Sugar, Three Styles:		
Cone Shaped, Round			As Creamer	12.50	12.50
Footed & Flat	12.50	11.50	Tumbler, 3½", 5 oz., Flat	20.00	18.00
Cup, Four Styles	6.50	6.50	Tumbler, 4", 5 oz., Footed	13.00	16.00
Goblet, 4", Cocktail	28.00	30.00	Tumbler, 9 oz., Flat	12.00	15.00
Goblet, 4½", Wine	28.00	30.00	Tumbler, 9 oz., Footed	14.00	16.00
Goblet, 5¾", 9 oz.	25.00	19.00	Tumbler, 10 oz., Flat	16.00	18.00
Ice Bucket	40.00	35.00	Tumbler, 6", 10 oz.,		
Ice Tub or Butter Tub, Open	80.00	35.00	Footed	20.00	24.00
Mug, Flat Creamer,			Tumbler, 14 oz., Flat	19.00	23.00
No Spout	----	30.00	Tumble-Up Night Set: 3"		
Pitcher, 7⅝", 68 oz.	60.00	65.00	Tumbler Bottle &		
Pitcher, 8½", 54 oz.	35.00	32.00	Tumbler, 6" High	----	55.00
Pitcher, 8", 80 oz.	65.00	55.00	Vase, 5¾", Blown	----	250.00
Plate, 6", Sherbet	2.50	2.50	Whiskey, 2¼", 2 oz.	24.00	24.00

17

"BOWKNOT"
(green)
UNKNOWN MANUFACTURER

	Green		Green
Bowl, 4½", Berry	13.00	Sherbet, Low Footed	13.00
Bowl, 5½", Cereal	16.00	Tumbler, 5", 10 oz.	16.00
Cup	7.00	Tumbler, 5", 10 oz. Footed	16.00
Plate, 7", Salad	10.00		

"BUBBLE," "FIRE KING"
(blue, dark green, ruby red, crystal)
HOCKING GLASS COMPANY, 1934–1965

	Crystal	Blue		Crystal	Blue
Bowl, 4", Berry	3.50	13.00	Platter, 12", Oval	5.00	15.00
Bowl, 4½", Fruit	4.00	10.00	Saucer	1.00	1.50
Bowl, 5¼", Cereal	5.00	12.00	Sugar	5.00	17.50
Bowl, 7¾", Flat Soup	6.00	14.00	Tumbler, 6 oz., Juice		
Bowl, 8⅜", Large Berry	6.00	15.00	(Red)	3.50	8.00
Creamer	5.00	30.00	Tumbler, 9 oz., Water		
Cup	3.00	3.00	(Red)	6.00	10.00
Pitcher, 64 oz., Ice Lip (Red)		50.00	Tumbler, 12 oz., Iced Tea		
Plate, 6¾", Bread & Butter	2.00	4.00	(Red)	10.00	12.50
Plate, 9⅜", Grill	----	18.00	Tumbler, 16 oz., Lemonade		
Plate, 9⅜", Dinner	5.00	6.50	(Red)	12.00	17.50

CAMEO, "BALLERINA," or "DANCING GIRL"
(green, yellow, pink and crystal with a platinum rim)
HOCKING GLASS COMPANY, 1930–1934

	Green	Yellow		Green	Yellow
Bowl, 4¾", Cream Soup ...	85.00	----	Decanter, 10" w/Stopper ..	125.00	----
Bowl, 5½", Cereal	28.00	26.00	Decanter, 10" w/Stopper,		
Bowl, 7¼", Salad	47.50	----	Frosted (Stoppers		
Bowl, 8¼", Large Berry ..	30.00	----	Represent ½ value of		
Bowl, 9", Rimmed Soup ...	40.00	----	Decanter	27.50	----
Bowl, 10", Oval Vegetable	20.00	35.00	Domino Tray, 7" w/3"		
Bowl, 11", Three-Leg			indentation	110.00	----
Console.......................	60.00	75.00	Goblet, 3½", Wine	550.00	----
Butter Dish & Cover	175.00	1,300.00	Goblet, 4", Wine	55.00	----
Cake Plate, 10",			Goblet, 6", Water	45.00	----
Three Legs.................	18.00	----	Ice Bowl or Open Butter		
Candlesticks, 4", Pr.	90.00	----	3" Tall x 5½" Wide ...	140.00	----
Candy Jar, Low 4" Cover	65.00	65.00	Jam Jar, 2" & Cover	140.00	----
Candy Jar, 6½" Tall &			Pitcher, 5¾", Syrup or		
Cover..........................	125.00	----	Milk, 20 oz................	170.00	2,000.00
Cocktail Shaker (Metal Lid)			Pitcher, 6", Juice, 36 oz.	50.00	----
Appears in Crystal Only	----	400.00	Pitcher, 8½", Water,		
Compote, 4" wide			56 oz.	45.00	----
Mayonnaise	26.00	----	Plate, 6", Sherbet	3.50	2.50
Cookie Jar & Cover......	45.00	----	Plate, 8", Luncheon	9.00	9.50
Creamer, 3¼"	19.00	16.00	Plate, 8½", Square	35.00	125.00
Creamer, 4¼"	22.50	----	Plate, 9½", Dinner	15.00	9.00
Cup, Two Styles	13.00	7.00	Plate, 10", Sandwich ...	12.00	----

	Green	Yellow		Green	Yellow
Plate, 10½", Grill	8.00	6.00	Sugar, 4¼"	21.00	----
Plate, 10½", Grill w/Closed Handles	60.00	6.00	Tumbler, 3¾", Juice, 5 oz.	25.00	----
Plate, 10½" w/Closed Handles	11.00	12.00	Tumbler, 4", Water, 9 oz.	22.00	----
Platter, 12" Closed Handles	17.50	35.00	Tumbler, 4¾", Flat, 10 oz.	23.00	----
Relish, 3-Part, 7½", Footed	25.00	150.00	Tumbler, 5", Flat, 11 oz.	25.00	42.00
Salt & Pepper, Footed, Pr.	60.00	----	Tumbler, 5¼", 15 oz.	57.50	----
Sandwich Server, Center Handle	3,500.00	----	Tumbler, Footed Juice, 3 oz.	50.00	----
Saucer w/Cup Ring	150.00	----	Tumbler, 5", Footed, 9 oz.	22.00	14.00
Saucer, 6" (Sherbet Plate)	4.00	3.00	Tumbler, 5¾", Footed, 11 oz.	50.00	----
Sherbet, 3⅛"	12.00	35.00	Vase, 5¾"	145.00	----
Sherbet, 4⅞"	30.00	37.50	Vase, 8"	25.00	----
Sugar, 3¼"	16.00	13.00	Water Bottle (Dark Green) Whitehouse Vinegar	15.00	----

CHERRYBERRY
(pink, green, iridescent)
U.S. GLASS COMPANY, 1928–1931

	Pink or Green		Pink or Green
Bowl, 4", Berry	8.00	Pickle Dish	14.00
Bowl, 6¼", 2" Deep	42.50	Pitcher, 7¾"	140.00
Bowl, 6½" Deep, Salad	17.50	Plate, 6", Sherbet	8.00
Bowl, 7½" Deep, Berry	19.50	Plate, 7½", Salad	13.00
Butter Dish & Cover	155.00	Sherbet	8.00
Compote, 5¾"	22.50	Sugar, Small, Open	16.00
Creamer, Small	16.00	Sugar, Large	22.00
Creamer, Large, 4⅝"	32.50	Sugar Cover	50.00
Olive Dish, 5", One Handle	14.00	Tumbler, 3⅝", 9 oz.	30.00

CHERRY BLOSSOM

(See Reproduction Section, Page 139–142) (pink, green, delphite, crystal)
JEANNETTE GLASS COMPANY, 1930–1939

	Pink	Green		Pink	Green
Bowl, 4¾", Berry	13.00	15.00	Saucer	5.00	5.00
Bowl, 5¾", Cereal	26.00	30.00	Sherbet	14.00	16.00
Bowl, 7¾", Flat Soup	47.50	47.50	Sugar	12.00	13.00
Bowl, 8½", Round Berry	40.00	40.00	Sugar Cover	14.00	15.00
Bowl, 9", Oval Vegetable	30.00	30.00	Tray, 10½", Sandwich,		
Bowl, 9", Two-Handled	25.00	27.50	Two Handled	16.00	19.00
Bowl, 10½", 3-Leg Fruit	67.50	67.50	Tumbler, 3¾", 4 oz., Footed		
Butter Dish & Cover	60.00	75.00	AOP, Round	13.50	16.00
Cake Plate (3 Legs) 10¼"	24.00	24.00	Tumbler, 4½", 9 oz., Round		
Coaster	12.00	10.00	Foot AOP	27.50	30.00
Creamer	16.00	16.00	Tumbler, 4½", 8 oz.,		
Cup	15.00	17.00	Scalloped Foot AOP	26.00	30.00
Mug, 7 oz.	180.00	155.00	Tumbler, 3½", 4 oz., Flat		
Pitcher, 6¾" AOP, 36 oz.			PAT	16.00	24.00
Scalloped or Round			Tumbler, 4¼", 9 oz., Flat		
Bottom	45.00	50.00	PAT	16.00	20.00
Pitcher, 8" PAT, 36 oz. Ftd.	48.00	48.00	Tumbler, 5", 12 oz., Flat PAT	47.50	60.00
Pitcher, 8" PAT, 42 oz. Flat	50.00	50.00			
Plate, 6", Sherbet	6.00	6.00			
Plate, 7", Salad	16.00	18.00			
Plate, 9", Dinner	18.00	20.00			
Plate, 9", Grill	20.00	22.00			
Platter, 9", Oval	750.00	900.00			
Platter, 11", Oval	30.00	35.00			
Platter, 13" & 13" Divided	55.00	55.00			
Salt & Pepper Scalloped					
Bottom	1,200.00	900.00			

CHILD'S JUNIOR DINNER SET

	Pink
Creamer	40.00
Sugar	40.00
Original box	15.00
Plate, 6"	9.00
Cup	32.50
Saucer	6.00
14-piece Set	280.00

CHINEX CLASSIC
(ivory, ivory decorated)
MacBETH-EVANS DIVISION OF CORNING GLASS WORKS
Late 1930–Early 1940s

	Ivory	Decorated		Ivory	Decorated
Bowl, 5¾", Cereal	5.00	7.50	Plate, 6¼", Sherbet	2.50	3.50
Bowl, 7", Salad	14.00	20.00	Plate, 9¾", Dinner	4.00	8.00
Bowl, 7¾", Flat Soup	12.00	16.00	Plate, 11½", Sandwich		
Bowl, 9", Vegetable	10.00	20.00	or Cake	7.50	13.00
Butter Dish	52.50	70.00	Saucer	2.00	3.00
Creamer	5.00	9.00	Sherbet, Low Footed	7.00	10.00
Cup	4.50	6.50	Sugar, Open	5.00	9.00

CHRISTMAS CANDY
(crystal, teal)
INDIANA GLASS COMPANY, 1950s

	Crystal	Teal		Crystal	Teal
Bowl, 7⅜", Soup	6.50	27.50	Plate, 9⅝", Dinner	9.50	27.50
Creamer	8.50	18.00	Plate, 11¼", Sandwich	13.50	37.50
Cup	4.50	18.00	Saucer	2.00	6.00
Plate, 6", Bread & Butter	3.00	10.00	Sugar	8.00	18.00
Plate, 8¼", Luncheon	6.50	16.00			

CIRCLE
(green, pink, crystal)
HOCKING GLASS COMPANY, 1930s

	Green or Pink		Green or Pink
Bowl, 4½"	8.00	Plate, 9½", Dinner	12.50
Bowl, 5½", Flared	10.00	Saucer	1.50
Bowl, 8"	15.00	Sherbet, 3⅛"	5.00
Creamer	8.50	Sherbet, 4¾"	6.00
Cup	4.50	Sugar	8.00
Goblet, 4½", Wine	12.00	Tumbler, 4 oz., Juice	8.00
Goblet, 8 oz., Water	10.00	Tumbler, 8 oz., Water	9.00
Pitcher, 80 oz.	30.00	Tumbler, 10 oz.	16.00
Plate, 6", Sherbet	2.00	Tumbler, 15 oz.	18.00
Plate, 8¼", Luncheon	4.00		

CLOVERLEAF
(pink, green, yellow, black)
HAZEL ATLAS GLASS COMPANY, 1930–1936

	Green	Yellow		Green	Yellow
Ashtray, 4", Match Holder in Center (black only)....	65.00	----	Plate, 6", Sherbet..............	4.50	6.50
Ashtray, 5¾", Match Holder in Center (black only)...............	77.50	----	Plate, 8", Luncheon	7.00	13.00
			Plate, 10¼", Grill	17.50	19.00
			Salt & Pepper, Pr.	27.50	95.00
			Saucer	3.50	4.50
Bowl, 4", Dessert	17.50	23.00	Sherbet, 3" Footed...........	6.50	10.00
Bowl, 5", Cereal	23.00	27.50	Sugar, Footed, 3⅝"..........	9.00	15.00
Bowl, 7", Salad	35.00	45.00	Tumbler, 3¾", 9 oz., Flat ...	35.00	----
Bowl, 8"	50.00	----	Tumbler, 4", 10 oz., Flat ...	30.00	----
Candy Dish & Cover	45.00	95.00	Tumbler, 5¾", 10 oz., Footed...........................	20.00	27.50
Creamer, Footed, 3⅝"	9.00	15.00			
Cup..................................	7.00	9.00			

COLONIAL, "KNIFE AND FORK"
(pink, green, crystal)
HOCKING GLASS COMPANY, 1934–1938

	Pink	Green
Bowl, 3¾"	40.00	----
Bowl, 4½", Berry	12.00	14.00
Bowl, 5½", Cereal	50.00	77.50
Bowl, 4½", Cream Soup	55.00	55.00
Bowl, 7", Low Soup	50.00	50.00
Bowl, 9", Large Berry	22.00	25.00
Bowl, 10", Oval Vegetable	25.00	28.00
Butter Dish & Cover	575.00	50.00
Creamer, 5", 8 oz., (Milk Pitcher)	40.00	20.00
Cup	10.00	10.00
Goblet, 3¾", 1 oz., Cordial	----	26.00
Goblet, 4", 3 oz., Cocktail	----	24.00
Goblet, 4½", 2½ oz., Wine	----	24.00
Goblet, 5¼", 4 oz., Claret	----	24.00
Goblet, 5¾", 8½ oz., Water	----	28.00
Mug, 4½", 12 oz.	450.00	750.00
Pitcher, 7", 54 oz., Ice Lip or None	45.00	47.50
Pitcher, 7¾", 68 oz., Ice Lip or None	55.00	60.00
Plate, 6", Sherbet	5.00	5.50
Plate, 8½", Luncheon	8.50	9.00
Plate, 10", Dinner	42.50	55.00
Plate, 10", Grill	22.00	24.00
Platter, 12", Oval	27.50	20.00
Salt & Pepper, Pr.	125.00	125.00
Saucer (Same as sherbet plate)	5.00	5.50
Sherbet	10.00	14.00
Spoon Holder or Celery	115.00	110.00
Sugar, 5"	22.50	12.00
Sugar Cover	45.00	18.00
Tumbler, 3", 5 oz., Juice	15.00	23.00
Tumbler, 4", 9 oz., Water	19.00	19.00
Tumbler, 10 oz.	33.00	38.00
Tumbler, 12 oz., Ice Tea	40.00	45.00
Tumbler, 15 oz., Lemonade	60.00	65.00
Tumbler, 3¼", 3 oz., Footed	13.00	20.00
Tumbler, 4", 5 oz., Footed	28.00	35.00
Tumbler, 5¼", 10 oz., Footed	40.00	45.00
Whiskey, 2½", 1½ oz	10.00	12.00

COLONIAL BLOCK
(green, pink, crystal, white)
HAZEL ATLAS GLASS COMPANY, Late 1920s–Early 1930s

	Green or Pink		Green or Pink
Bowl, 4"	6.00	Creamer	10.00
Bowl, 7"	16.00	Pitcher	35.00
Butter Dish	42.50	Sugar	10.00
Butter Tub	32.50	Sugar Cover	10.00
Candy Dish & Cover, 8½"	32.50		

COLONIAL FLUTED, "ROPE"
(green, crystal)
FEDERAL GLASS COMPANY, 1928–1933

	Green		Green
Bowl, 4", Berry	5.00	Plate, 6", Sherbet	2.00
Bowl, 6", Cereal	7.50	Plate, 8", Luncheon	5.00
Bowl, 6½", Deep Salad	17.50	Saucer	1.50
Bowl, 7½", Large Berry	15.00	Sherbet	6.00
Creamer	6.00	Sugar	5.00
Cup	4.50	Sugar Cover	15.00

COLUMBIA
(crystal, pink)
FEDERAL GLASS COMPANY, 1938–1942

	Crystal	Pink		Crystal	Pink
Bowl, 5", Cereal	14.00	----	Plate, 9½", Luncheon	8.50	25.00
Bowl, 8", Low Soup	16.00	----	Plate, 11¾", Chop	9.00	----
Bowl, 8½", Salad	16.00	----	Saucer	3.00	8.00
Bowl, 10½", Ruffled Edge	18.00	----	Snack Plate	35.00	----
Butter Dish & Cover	15.00	----	Tumbler, 4 oz.	16.00	----
Cup	8.00	18.00	Tumbler, 9 oz.	22.00	----
Plate, 6", Bread & Butter	3.00	12.00			

CORONATION, "BANDED FINE RIB," "SAXON"
(pink, crystal, royal ruby)
HOCKING GLASS COMPANY, 1936–1940

	Pink	Red		Pink	Red
Bowl, 4¼", Berry	4.00	6.00	Plate, 8½", Luncheon	4.00	8.00
Bowl, 6½", Nappy	6.00	10.00	Saucer	2.00	----
Bowl, 8", Large Berry	7.00	15.00	Sherbet	4.00	----
Cup	5.00	6.00	Tumbler, 5", 10 oz.,		
Pitcher, 7¾", 68 oz.	200.00	----	Footed	18.00	----
Plate, 6", Sherbet	1.50	----			

CREMAX
(cremax, decal decorations)
MacBETH-EVANS DIVISION OF CORNING GLASS WORKS
Late 1930s – Early 1940s

	Ivory	Ivory Decorated		Ivory	Ivory Decorated
Bowl, 5¾", Cereal	3.00	7.00	Plate, 9¾", Dinner	4.00	9.00
Bowl, 9", Vegetable	6.00	12.50	Plate, 11½", Sandwich	4.50	10.00
Creamer	4.50	7.50	Saucer	2.00	3.00
Cup	4.00	4.50	Sugar, Open	4.50	7.50
Plate, 6¼", Bread & Butter	2.00	3.50			

CUBE, "CUBIST"
(pink, green, crystal)
JEANNETTE GLASS COMPANY, 1929–1933

	Pink	Green		Pink	Green
Bowl, 4½", Dessert	5.50	6.00	Plate, 8", Luncheon	5.00	6.00
Bowl, 4½" Deep	6.50	----	Powder Jar & Cover,		
Bowl, 6½", Salad	8.50	13.00	Three Legs	22.00	22.00
Butter Dish & Cover	55.00	55.00	Salt & Pepper, Pr.	32.50	30.00
Candy Jar & Cover, 6½"	25.00	28.00	Saucer	2.50	3.50
Coaster, 3¼"	6.00	6.50	Sherbet, Footed	6.50	7.00
Creamer, 2"	2.00	----	Sugar, 2"	2.00	----
Creamer, 3"	6.00	8.00	Sugar, 3"	6.00	7.00
Cup	6.50	8.00	Sugar/Candy Cover	12.00	12.00
Pitcher, 8¾", 45 oz.	180.00	200.00	Tumbler, 4", 9 oz.	55.00	55.00
Plate, 6" Sherbet	3.00	3.00			

"DAISY," NUMBER 620
(crystal, 1933; amber, 1940; dark green and milk glass, 1960s)
INDIANA GLASS COMPANY

	Crystal	Amber		Crystal	Amber
Bowl, 4½", Berry	4.50	8.50	Plate, 9⅜", Dinner	5.00	9.00
Bowl, 4½", Cream Soup	4.00	12.00	Plate, 10⅜", Grill	4.00	9.50
Bowl, 6", Cereal	10.00	25.00	Plate, 11½", Cake or		
Bowl, 7⅜", Berry	7.00	14.00	Sandwich	6.00	12.00
Bowl, 9⅜", Deep Berry	13.00	30.00	Platter, 10¾"	7.00	14.00
Bowl, 10", Oval Vegetable	9.00	15.00	Relish Dish, 3 Part, 8⅜"	12.00	30.00
Creamer, Footed	5.00	8.00	Saucer	1.50	2.00
Cup	4.00	6.00	Sherbet, Footed	4.50	8.50
Plate, 6", Sherbet	2.00	3.00	Sugar, Footed	5.00	8.00
Plate, 7⅜", Salad	3.00	7.00	Tumbler, 9 oz., Footed	9.00	18.00
Plate, 8⅜", Luncheon	4.00	6.00	Tumbler, 12 oz., Footed	19.00	35.00

DIAMOND QUILTED, "FLAT DIAMOND"
(pink, blue, green, crystal, black)
IMPERIAL GLASS COMPANY, Late 1920s – Early 1930s

	Green	Blue		Green	Blue
Bowl, 4¾", Cream Soup ...	7.50	17.00	Mayonnaise Set: Ladle,		
Bowl, 5", Cereal	6.50	13.00	Plate, Three-Footed Dish	35.00	----
Bowl, 5½", One Handle	6.00	15.00	Pitcher, 64 oz.	45.00	----
Bowl, 7", Crimped Edge ...	7.00	15.00	Plate, 6", Sherbet	3.50	5.00
Bowl, Rolled Edge Console ..	18.00	50.00	Plate, 7", Salad	5.00	8.00
Cake Salver, Tall, 10"			Plate, 8", Luncheon	5.00	11.00
Diameter	50.00	----	Plate, 14", Sandwich	12.00	----
Candlesticks (2 styles), Pr.	22.00	45.00	Punch Bowl & Stand	380.00	----
Candy Jar & Cover,			Sandwich Server, Center		
Footed............................	55.00	----	Handle	22.00	45.00
Compote & Cover, 11½" ...	65.00	----	Saucer	2.50	5.00
Creamer	7.50	16.00	Sherbet..............................	4.50	14.00
Cup	9.00	15.00	Sugar.................................	7.50	14.00
Goblet, 1 oz. Cordial	10.00	----	Tumbler, 9 oz., Water	8.00	----
Goblet, 2 oz. Wine	10.00	----	Tumbler, 12 oz., Ice Tea .	9.00	----
Goblet, 3 oz, Wine	10.00	----	Tumbler, 6 oz., Footed	8.50	----
Goblet, 6", 9 oz.,			Tumbler, 9 oz., Footed	12.00	----
Champagne	9.00	----	Tumbler, 12 oz., Footed ...	14.00	----
Ice Bucket	45.00	75.00	Whiskey, 1½ oz.	8.00	----

DIANA
(pink, amber, crystal)
FEDERAL GLASS COMPANY, 1937–1941

	Pink	Amber		Pink	Amber
Ashtray, 3½"	3.50	----	Plate, 6", Bread & Butter ...	4.00	2.00
Bowl, 5", Cereal	8.00	----	Plate, 9½", Dinner	12.00	8.00
Bowl, 5½", Cream Soup	18.00	12.00	Plate, 11¾", Sandwich	20.00	9.00
Bowl, 9", Salad	18.00	6.50	Platter, 12", Oval	25.00	12.00
Bowl, 11", Console Fruit	32.50	12.00	Salt & Pepper, Pr.	60.00	90.00
Bowl, 12", Scalloped Edge	22.50	15.00	Saucer	4.00	2.00
Candy Jar & Cover, Round	35.00	30.00	Sherbet	10.00	12.00
Coaster, 3½"	7.00	----	Sugar, Open, Oval	10.00	7.00
Creamer, Oval	10.00	8.00	Tumbler, 4⅛", 9 oz.	40.00	23.00
Cup	11.00	6.00			
Cup, Demitasse, 2 oz. & 4½" Saucer Set	40.00	----			

DOGWOOD, "APPLE BLOSSOM," "WILD ROSE"
(pink, green)
MacBETH EVANS COMPANY, 1929–1932

	Pink	Green
Bowl, 5½", Cereal	22.00	22.00
Bowl, 8½", Berry	47.50	90.00
Bowl, 10¼", Fruit	175.00	175.00
Cake Plate, 11", Heavy Solid Foot	225.00	----
Cake Plate, 13", Heavy Solid Foot	77.50	70.00
Creamer, 2½", Thin	15.00	40.00
Creamer, 3¼", Thick	18.00	----
Cup, Thin or Thick	12.00	32.00
Pitcher, 8", 80 oz., Decorated	145.00	450.00
Pitcher, 8", 80 oz., (American Sweetheart Style)	525.00	----
Plate, 6", Bread & Butter	7.00	7.00
Plate, 8", Luncheon	6.50	7.00

	Pink	Green
Plate, 9¼", Dinner	25.00	----
Plate, 10½", Grill AOP or Border Design Only	18.00	17.00
Plate, 12", Salver	23.00	----
Platter, 12", Oval (Rare)	350.00	----
Saucer	6.00	6.50
Sherbet, Low Footed	27.50	85.00
Sugar, 2½", Thin	15.00	40.00
Sugar, 3¼", Thick	14.00	----
Tumbler, 3½", 5 oz., Decorated	250.00	----
Tumbler, 4", 10 oz., Decorated	32.50	70.00
Tumbler, 4¾", 11 oz., Decorated	37.50	80.00
Tumbler, 5", 12 oz., Decorated	45.00	90.00

DORIC
(pink, green)
JEANNETTE GLASS COMPANY, 1935–1938

	Pink	Green		Pink	Green
Bowl, 4½", Berry	6.00	7.00	Plate, 6", Sherbet	3.50	4.50
Bowl, 5", 2 Handled			Plate, 7", Salad	15.00	16.00
Cream Soup	----	300.00	Plate, 9", Dinner	10.00	14.00
Bowl, 5½", Cereal	40.00	55.00	Plate, 9", Grill	12.00	15.00
Bowl, 8¼", Large Berry	12.00	15.00	Platter, 12", Oval	18.00	20.00
Bowl, 9", Two Handled	12.00	13.00	Relish Tray, 4" x 4"	8.00	8.00
Bowl, 9", Oval Vegetable	20.00	25.00	Relish Tray, 4" x 8"	10.00	14.00
Butter Dish & Cover	60.00	75.00	Salt & Pepper, Pr.	30.00	32.50
Cake Plate, 10", 3 Legs	20.00	25.00	Saucer	3.00	3.50
Candy Dish & Cover, 8"	30.00	32.50	Sherbet, Footed	10.00	12.00
Candy Dish, Three Part	5.00	6.00	Sugar	10.00	11.00
Coaster, 3"	15.00	15.00	Sugar Cover	12.00	20.00
Creamer, 4"	10.00	13.00	Tray, 10", Handled	12.00	13.00
Cup	7.00	8.00	Tray, 8" x 8", Serving	18.00	20.00
Pitcher, 6", 36 oz., Flat	25.00	35.00	Tumbler, 4½", 9 oz., Flat	50.00	85.00
Pitcher, 7½", 48 oz., Ftd.	400.00	750.00	Tumbler, 4", 10 oz., Ftd.	50.00	75.00
			Tumbler, 5", 12 oz., Ftd.	65.00	95.00

DORIC AND PANSY
(pink, crystal, ultramarine)
JEANNETTE GLASS COMPANY, 1937–1938

	Pink	Ultramarine
Bowl, 4½", Berry	7.00	15.00
Bowl, 8", Large Berry	18.00	70.00
Bowl, 9", Handled	14.00	30.00
Butter Dish & Cover	----	450.00
Cup	----	16.00
Creamer	----	115.00
Plate, 6", Sherbet	7.00	9.00
Plate, 7", Salad	----	30.00
Plate, 9", Dinner	----	25.00
Salt & Pepper, Pr.	----	350.00
Saucer	----	5.00
Sugar, Open	----	110.00
Tray, 10", Handled	----	20.00
Tumbler, 4½", 9 oz.	----	65.00

"PRETTY POLLY PARTY DISHES"

	Pink	Ultramarine
Cup	27.50	37.50
Saucer	5.00	6.00
Plate	7.00	9.00
Creamer	27.50	37.50
Sugar	27.50	37.50
14-Piece Set	200.00	285.00

ENGLISH HOBNAIL
(crystal, pink, amber, turquoise, cobalt, green)
WESTMORELAND GLASS COMPANY, 1920s–1970s

	Pink or Green		Pink or Green
Ashtray, Several Shapes	20.00	Goblet, 6¼", 8 oz.	22.50
Bowls, 4½", 5" Square & Round	10.00	Grapefruit, 6½", Flange Rim	16.00
Bowl, Cream Soup	14.00	Lamp, 6¼", Electric	45.00
Bowls, 6", Several Styles	12.00	Lamp, 9¼"	95.00
Bowls, 8", Several Styles	23.00	Marmalade & Cover	36.00
Bowls, 8", Footed & Two-Handled	50.00	Pitcher, 23 oz.	145.00
Bowls, 11" & 12" Nappies	40.00	Pitcher, 39 oz.	175.00
Bowls, Relish, Oval, 8" & 9"	18.00	Pitcher, 60 oz.	210.00
Bowl, Relish, Oval, 12"	20.00	Pitcher, ½ Gal., Straight Sides	235.00
Candlesticks, 3½", Pr.	35.00	Plate, 5½" & 6½", Sherbet	5.00
Candlesticks, 8½", Pr.	55.00	Plate, 7¼", Pie	5.00
Candy Dish, ½ lb., Cone Shaped	50.00	Plate, 8", Round or Square	8.00
Candy Dish & Cover, Three Feet	70.00	Plate, 10", Dinner	22.50
Celery Dish, 9"	21.00	Salt & Pepper, Pr., Round or Sq. Base	77.50
Celery Dish, 12"	26.00	Salt Dip, 2" Footed & w/Place	
Cigarette Box	30.00	Card Holder	22.00
Cologne Bottle	30.00	Saucer	4.00
Creamer, Footed or Flat	22.00	Sherbet	14.00
Cup	16.00	Sugar, Footed or Flat	24.00
Decanter, 20 oz. w/Stopper	98.00	Tumbler, 3¾", 5 oz. or 8 oz	14.00
Demitasse Cup & Saucer	50.00	Tumbler, 4", 10 oz. Ice Tea	16.00
Egg Cup	36.00	Tumbler, 5", 12 oz. Ice Tea	24.00
Goblet, 1 oz. Cordial	25.00	Tumbler, 7 oz., Footed	15.00
Goblet, 2 oz. Wine	22.00	Tumbler, 9 oz., Footed	16.00
Goblet, 3 oz. Cocktail	17.00	Tumbler, 12½ oz., Footed	22.50
Goblet, 5 oz. Claret	20.00	Whiskey, 1½ & 3 oz.	25.00

FIRE-KING DINNERWARE, "ALICE"
ANCHOR HOCKING COMPANY, 1940s

	White/trim Jade-ite		White/trim Jade-ite
Cup	7.50	Saucer	2.50
Plate	15.00		

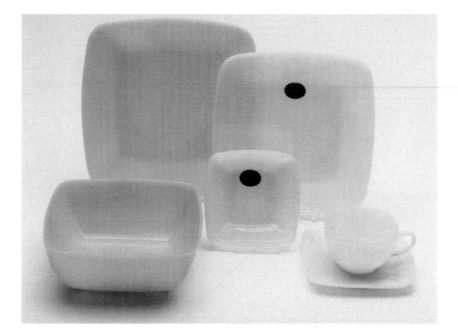

FIRE-KING DINNERWARE, CHARM
ANCHOR HOCKING GLASS CORPORATION, 1940s–1960s

	Azur-ite	Jade-ite		Azur-ite	Jade-ite
Bowl, 4¾", Dessert	6.50	4.00	Plate, 6⅝", Salad	4.00	3.00
Bowl, 6", Soup	20.00	12.00	Plate, 8⅜", Luncheon	7.50	4.50
Bowl, 7⅜", Salad	12.50	7.50	Plate, 10", Dinner	20.00	12.00
Creamer	9.50	6.00	Platter	20.00	10.00
Cup	6.50	3.00	Saucer	1.50	1.00
			Sugar	9.50	6.00

FIRE-KING DINNERWARE, "JANE RAY"
ANCHOR HOCKING COMPANY, 1945–1960s

	Jade-ite
Bowl, 4⅞", Dessert	4.00
Bowl, 5⅞", Oatmeal	6.00
Bowl, 7⅝", Soup	12.00
Bowl, 8¼", Vegetable	12.50
Cup	2.00
Cup, demitasse	12.50
Creamer	4.00

	Jade-ite
Plate, 7¾", Salad	5.00
Plate, 9⅛", Dinner	6.00
Platter, 12"	11.00
Saucer	1.00
Saucer, demitasse	12.50
Sugar	4.00
Sugar Cover	5.00

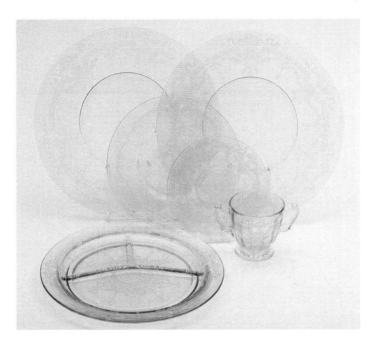

FIRE-KING DINNERWARE, "PHILBE"
(blue, pink, green and crystal)
ANCHOR HOCKING GLASS COMPANY, 1937–1938

	Pink or Green		Pink or Green
Bowl, 5½", Cereal	35.00	Plate, 10½", Salver	40.00
Bowl, 7¼", Salad	45.00	Plate, 10½", Grill	35.00
Bowl, 10", Oval Vegetable	50.00	Plate, 11⅝", Salver	40.00
Candy Jar, 4", Low w/Cover	700.00	Platter, 12", Closed Handles	100.00
Cookie Jar w/Cover	750.00	Saucer, 6" (same as sherbet plate)	35.00
Creamer, 3¼", Footed	100.00	Sugar, 3¼", Footed	100.00
Cup	100.00	Tumbler, 4", 9 oz., Flat Water	100.00
Goblet, 7¼", Thin, 9 oz.	160.00	Tumbler, 3½", Footed Juice	150.00
Pitcher, 6", Juice, 36 oz.	550.00	Tumbler, 5¼", Footed, 10 oz.	50.00
Pitcher, 8½", 54 oz.	750.00	Tumbler, 6½", Footed, 15 oz. Ice Tea	45.00
Plate, 6", Sherbet	35.00		
Plate, 8", Luncheon	30.00		
Plate, 10", Heavy Sandwich	40.00		

FIRE-KING OVEN GLASS
(blue, 1940s; crystal, 1950s)
ANCHOR HOCKING GLASS COMPANY

	Blue		Blue
Baker, 1 Pt., Round or Square	5.00	Loaf Pan, 9⅛" Deep	20.00
Baker, 1 Qt.	6.50	Nurser, 4 oz.	14.00
Baker, 1½ Qt.	11.00	Nurser, 8 oz.	22.50
Baker, 2 Qt.	12.50	Pie Plate, 4⅜", Individual	10.00
Cake Pan (deep), 8¾"	20.00	Pie Plate, 5⅜", Deep Dish	11.00
Casserole, 1 Pt., Knob Handle		Pie Plate, 8⅜"	7.00
Cover	11.00	Pie Plate, 9"	9.00
Casserole, 1 Qt., Knob Handle		Pie Plate, 9⅝"	9.00
Cover	12.00	Pie Plate, 10⅜", Juice Saver	65.00
Casserole, 1½ Qt., Knob Handle		Perculator Top, 2⅛"	3.50
Cover	13.00	Refrigerator Jar & Cover, 4½" x 5" ...	10.00
Casserole, 2 Qt., Knob Handle		Refrigerator Jar & Cover,	
Cover	20.00	5⅛" x 9⅛"	27.50
Casserole, 1 Qt., Pie Plate Cover ...	18.00	Roaster, 8¾"	37.50
Casserole, 1½ Qt., Pie Plate		Roaster, 10⅜"	65.00
Cover	20.00	Table Server, Tab Handles	
Casserole, 2 Qt., Pie Plate Cover	25.00	(Hot Plate)	15.00
Casserole, 10 oz., Tab Handle		Utility Bowl, 6⅞"	10.00
Cover	15.00	Utility Bowl, 8⅜"	14.00
Coffee Mug, 7 oz.	22.00	Utility Bowl, 10⅛"	18.00
Cup, 8 oz., Measuring	16.00	Utility Pan, 10½", Rectangular	17.50
Custard Cup, 5 oz.	3.00	Utility Pan, 8⅛" x 12½"	19.00
Custard Cup, 6 oz., Two Styles	3.50		

FIRE-KING OVEN WARE TURQUOISE BLUE
(turquoise blue)
ANCHOR HOCKING GLASS CORPORATION, 1950s

	Blue		Blue
Bowl, 4½", Berry	5.00	Creamer	5.00
Bowl, 5", Cereal	8.50	Cup	4.00
Bowl, 6⅝", Soup/Salad	12.50	Mug, 8 oz.	10.00
Bowl, 8", Vegetable	14.00	Plate, 6⅛"	10.00
Bowl, Tear, Mixing, 1 Pt.	10.00	Plate, 7"	9.00
Bowl, Tear, Mixing, 1 Qt.	12.00	Plate, 9"	7.00
Bowl, Tear, Mixing, 2 Qt.	15.00	Plate, 9" w/Cup Indent	6.00
Bowl, Tear, Mixing, 3 Qt.	18.00	Plate, 10"	25.00
Bowl, Round, Mixing, 1 Qt.	10.00	Relish, 3-Part	11.00
Bowl, Round, Mixing, 2 Qt.	8.00	Saucer	1.00
Bowl, Round, Mixing, 3 Qt.	10.00	Sugar	5.00
Bowl, Round, Mixing, 4 Qt.	12.50		

FIRE-KING OVEN WARE "SWIRL"
(blue, pink, white w/gold trim, ivory w/trims, jade-ite)
ANCHOR HOCKING GLASS CORPORATION, 1955–1960s

	Jade-ite	Azur-ite		Jade-ite	Azur-ite
Bowl, Berry, 4⅞"	2.50	4.00	Platter, 12"	7.50	13.00
Creamer	3.50	6.50	Saucer	.50	1.00
Cup	3.00	4.50	Sugar	2.50	5.50
Plate, 7¾", Salad	2.50	3.50	Sugar Cover	3.50	4.50
Plate, 9⅛", Dinner	4.00	6.00			

FLORAGOLD, "LOUISA"
(iridescent, shell pink, crystal)
JEANNETTE GLASS COMPANY, 1950s

	Iridescent
Bowl, 4½", Square	5.00
Bowl, 5½", Cereal, Round	30.00
Bowl, 5½", Ruffled Fruit	8.00
Bowl, 8½", Square	12.50
Bowl, 9½", Salad, Deep	35.00
Bowl, 9½", Ruffled	7.50
Bowl, 12", Ruffled, Large Fruit	6.50
Butter Dish & Cover, ¼ lb., Oblong	22.50
Butter Dish & Cover, Round	40.00
Candlesticks, Double Branch, Pr.	45.00
Candy or Cheese Dish & Cover, 6¾"	45.00
Candy, 5¼" Long, 4 Feet	7.00
Coaster/Ashtray, 4"	5.00
Creamer	8.50

	Iridescent
Cup	5.50
Pitcher, 64 oz.	32.50
Plate, 5¾", Sherbet	10.00
Plate, 8½", Dinner	30.00
Plate or Tray, 13½"	17.50
Indent on 13½" Plate	45.00
Platter, 11¼"	17.50
Salt & Pepper, Plastic Tops	45.00
Saucer (same as sherbet plate)	10.00
Sherbet, Low Footed	12.50
Sugar	6.00
Sugar Lid	9.50
Tumbler, 10 oz., Footed	17.50
Tumbler, 11 oz., Footed	17.50
Tumbler, 15 oz., Footed	85.00
Vase or Celery	335.00

FLORAL, "POINSETTIA"
(See Reproduction Section, Page 143)
(pink, green, delphite)
JEANNETTE GLASS COMPANY, 1931–1935

	Pink	Green
Bowl, 4", Berry	14.00	15.00
Bowl, 5½", Cream Soup	675.00	675.00
Bowl, 7½", Salad	15.00	15.00
Bowl, 8", Covered Vegetable	30.00	37.50
Bowl, 9", Oval Vegetable	15.00	15.00
Butter Dish & Cover	77.50	80.00
Candlesticks, 4", Pr.	65.00	75.00
Candy Jar & Cover	30.00	35.00
Coaster, 3¼"	12.00	8.00
Compote, 9"	650.00	750.00
Creamer, Flat	12.00	13.00
Cup	10.00	11.00
Ice Tub, 3½" High, Oval	650.00	675.00
Lamp	230.00	250.00
Pitcher, 5½", 23 or 24 oz., Flat	----	475.00
Pitcher, 8", 32 oz., Footed Cone	30.00	32.00
Pitcher, 10¼", 48 oz., Lemonade	200.00	225.00
Plate, 6", Sherbet	5.00	7.00
Plate, 8", Salad	9.00	10.00
Plate, 9", Dinner	14.00	16.00

	Pink	Green
Plate, 9", Grill	----	155.00
Platter, 10¾", Oval	15.00	15.00
Refrigerator Dish & Cover, 5" Square	----	65.00
Relish Dish, Oval, Two-Part	14.00	14.00
Salt & Pepper, 4", Footed, Pr. *(Beware reproductions)*	40.00	47.50
Salt & Pepper, 6" Flat	45.00	----
Saucer	9.00	10.00
Sherbet	14.00	16.00
Sugar	8.00	10.00
Sugar/Candy Cover	15.00	15.00
Tray, 6" Square, Closed Handles	12.50	15.00
Tumbler, 4", 5 oz., Footed Juice	15.00	18.00
Tumbler, 4¾", 7 oz., Footed Water	16.00	19.00
Tumbler, 5¼", 9 oz., Footed Lemonade	40.00	42.00
Vase, 3-Legged Rose Bowl	----	450.00
Vase, 3-Legged Flared (Also in Crystal)	----	450.00
Vase, 6⅞" Tall (8-sided)	----	400.00

FLORAL AND DIAMOND BAND
(crystal, pink, green)
U.S. GLASS COMPANY, 1927–1931

	Pink	Green		Pink	Green
Bowl, 4½", Berry	7.00	8.00	Pitcher, 8", 42 oz.	85.00	90.00
Bowl, 5¾", Nappy,			Plate, 8", Luncheon	30.00	30.00
Handled	10.00	10.00	Sherbet	6.00	7.00
Bowl, 8", Large Berry	12.00	13.00	Sugar, Small	9.00	10.00
Butter Dish & Cover	125.00	110.00	Sugar, 5¼"	13.00	13.00
Compote, 5½" Tall	14.00	15.00	Sugar Lid	45.00	55.00
Creamer, Small	9.00	10.00	Tumbler, 4", Water	18.00	22.00
Creamer, 4¾"	16.00	18.00	Tumbler, 5", Ice Tea	30.00	35.00

FLORENTINE NO. 1, "POPPY NO. 1"
(See Reproduction Section, Page 143)
(pink, green, crystal, yellow, cobalt)
HAZEL ATLAS GLASS COMPANY, 1934–1936

	Green	Yellow		Green	Yellow
Ashtray, 5½"	20.00	26.00	Plate, 8½", Salad	7.00	11.00
Bowl, 5", Berry	10.00	13.00	Plate, 10", Dinner	14.00	20.00
Bowl, 6", Cereal	20.00	20.00	Plate, 10", Grill	10.00	13.00
Bowl, 8½", Large Berry	20.00	25.00	Platter, 11½", Oval	13.00	19.00
Bowl, 9½", Oval Vegetable			* Salt & Pepper, Footed	35.00	50.00
& Cover	45.00	55.00	Saucer	3.00	4.00
Butter Dish & Cover	120.00	150.00	Sherbet, 3 oz., Footed	9.00	11.00
Coaster/Ashtray, 3¾"	15.00	18.00	Sugar	9.00	12.00
Creamer	9.00	11.00	Sugar Cover	15.00	20.00
Creamer, Ruffled	35.00	----	Sugar, Ruffled	30.00	----
Cup	8.50	9.50	Tumbler, 3¾", 5 oz.,		
Pitcher, 6½", 36 oz.,			Footed Juice	13.00	19.00
Footed	37.50	45.00	Tumbler, 4¾", 10 oz.,		
Pitcher, 7½", 54 oz., Flat			Footed Water	20.00	18.00
Ice Lip or None	60.00	160.00	Tumbler, 5¼", 12 oz.,		
Plate, 6", Sherbet	5.00	6.00	Footed Ice Tea	25.00	28.00

* Beware reproductions

FLORENTINE NO. 2, "POPPY NO. 2"
(pink, green, yellow, crystal, cobalt blue)
HAZEL ATLAS GLASS COMPANY, 1932–1935

	Green	Yellow
Bowl, 4½", Berry	10.00	17.00
Bowl, 4¾", Cream Soup	12.00	19.00
Bowl, 5¼"	30.00	35.00
Bowl, 6", Cereal	25.00	35.00
Bowl, 8", Large Berry	19.00	25.00
Bowl, 9", Oval Vegetable & Cover	45.00	55.00
Butter Dish & Cover	95.00	135.00
Candlesticks, 2¾", Pr.	40.00	55.00
Candy Dish & Cover	95.00	135.00
Coaster, 3¼"	12.00	20.00
Coaster/Ashtray, 3¾"	16.00	20.00
Coaster/Ashtray, 5½"	17.00	32.00
Compote, 3½", Ruffled	20.00	----
Creamer	7.50	9.50
Cup	7.00	8.00
Custard Cup or Jello	55.00	75.00
Gravy Boat	----	47.50
Pitcher, 7½", 28 oz., Cone Footed	28.00	29.00
Pitcher, 7½", 54 oz.	50.00	145.00
Pitcher, 8", 76 oz.	85.00	350.00
Plate, 6", Sherbet	3.00	5.00

	Green	Yellow
Plate, 6¼", w/Indent for Custard	15.00	25.00
Plate, 8½", Salad	7.00	8.00
Plate, 10", Dinner	13.00	13.00
Plate, 10¼", Grill	10.00	10.00
Platter, 11", Oval	15.00	18.00
Platter, 11½" for Gravy Boat	----	35.00
Relish Dish, 10", 3 Part or Plain	18.00	25.00
Salt & Pepper, Pr.	40.00	46.00
Saucer	3.00	4.00
Sherbet, Footed	9.00	10.00
Sugar	8.00	9.00
Sugar Cover	13.00	20.00
Tumbler, 3½", 5 oz., Juice	10.00	19.00
Tumbler, 4", 9 oz. Water	11.00	18.00
Tumbler, 5", 12 oz., Ice Tea	30.00	40.00
Tumbler, 3¼", 5 oz., Footed	13.00	15.00
Tumbler, 4", 5 oz., Footed	13.00	15.00
Tumbler, 4½", 9 oz., Footed	20.00	30.00
Vase or Parfait, 6"	28.00	55.00

FLOWER GARDEN WITH BUTTERFLIES, "BUTTERFLIES AND ROSES"
(pink, green, blue-green, canary yellow, amber, black)
U.S. GLASS COMPANY, Late 1920s

	Pink or Green		Pink or Green
Ashtray, Match-Pack Holders	165.00	Plate, 8", Two Styles	16.00
Bowl, Rolled Edge Console	75.00	Plate, Dinner, 10"	40.00
Candlesticks, 4", Pr.	50.00	Powder Jar, Footed	100.00
Candlesticks, 8", Pr.	135.00	Powder Jar, Flat	60.00
Candy Dish & Cover, 7½"	125.00	Sandwich Server, Center Handle	60.00
Candy Dish, Open, 6"	25.00	Saucer	25.00
Cheese & Cracker Set (4" Compote, 10" Plate)	65.00	Sugar, Open	65.00
Cologne Bottle, 7½", Tall Footed	160.00	Tray, 5½" x 10", Oval	50.00
Console Bowl, 10" Footed	85.00	Tray, Rectangular, 11¾" x 7¾"	60.00
Creamer	65.00	Vase, 7", (black)	125.00
Cup	60.00	Vase, 10"	125.00

FOREST GREEN
(dark green glass)
ANCHOR HOCKING, 1950s–1967

	Green		Green
Ashtray	3.50	Pitcher, 3 Qt., Round	25.00
Bowl, 4¾", Dessert	5.00	Platter, Rectangular	25.00
Bowl, 6", Soup	15.00	Saucer	1.50
Bowl, 7⅜", Salad	12.50	Sugar, Flat	6.00
Creamer, Flat	6.00	Tumbler, 5 oz.	3.50
Cup	4.00	Tumbler, 10 oz.	6.50
Plate, 6⅝", Salad	4.00	Vase, 4", Ivy	3.00
Plate, 8⅜", Luncheon	5.00	Vase, 6⅜"	4.00
Plate, 10", Dinner	25.00	Vase, 9"	6.00

"FORTUNE"
(pink, crystal)
HOCKING GLASS COMPANY, 1937–1938

	Pink		Pink
Bowl, 4", Berry	3.50	Cup	4.00
Bowl, 4½", Dessert	4.00	Plate, 6", Sherbet	2.50
Bowl, 4½", Handled	4.00	Plate, 8", Luncheon	8.50
Bowl, 5¼", Rolled Edge	6.00	Saucer	2.50
Bowl, 7¾", Salad or Large Berry	12.00	Tumbler, 3½", Juice, 5 oz.	6.50
Candy Dish & Cover, Flat	22.50	Tumbler, 4", Water, 9 oz.	8.50

"FRUITS"
(pink, green, crystal)
HAZEL ATLAS AND OTHER GLASS COMPANIES, 1931–1953

	Pink	Green		Pink	Green
Bowl, 5", Cereal	20.00	20.00	Sherbet	6.00	7.50
Bowl, 8", Berry	36.00	50.00	Tumbler, 3½", Juice	15.00	20.00
Cup	6.00	7.00	Tumbler, 4" (One Fruit)	12.00	15.00
Pitcher, 7", Flat Bottom	----	65.00	Tumbler, 4" (Combination		
Plate, 8", Luncheon	6.00	6.00	of Fruits)	20.00	25.00
Saucer	4.00	5.00	Tumbler, 5", 12 oz.	----	95.00

GEORGIAN, "LOVEBIRDS"
(green, crystal)
FEDERAL GLASS COMPANY, 1931–1936

	Green		Green
Bowl, 4½", Berry	7.50	Plate, 6", Sherbet	5.00
Bowl, 5¾", Cereal	20.00	Plate, 8", Luncheon	8.00
Bowl, 6½", Deep	60.00	Plate, 9¼", Dinner	24.00
Bowl, 7½", Large Berry	55.00	Plate, 9¼", Center Design Only	19.00
Bowl, 9", Oval Vegetable	55.00	Platter, 11½", Closed Handled	57.50
Butter Dish & Cover	72.50	Saucer	4.00
Cold Cuts Server, 18½", Wood w/Seven 5" Openings for 5" Coasters	750.00	Sherbet	11.00
Creamer, 3", Footed	10.00	Sugar, 3", Footed	8.50
Creamer, 4", Footed	13.00	Sugar, 4", Footed	9.50
Cup	8.50	Sugar Cover, 3"	30.00
Hot Plate, 5" Center Design	42.50	Sugar Cover, 4"	82.00
		Tumbler, 4", Flat, 9 oz.	47.50
		Tumbler, 5¼", Flat, 12 oz.	97.50

HARP
(crystal and crystal with gold rims)
JEANNETTE GLASS COMPANY, 1954–1957

	Crystal		Crystal
Ashtray/Coaster	4.50	Plate, 7"	10.00
Coaster	3.50	Saucer	5.00
Cup	12.50	Tray, Rectangular	30.00
Cake Stand, 9"	22.50	Vase, 6"	17.50

HERITAGE
(crystal, pink, blue, green)
FEDERAL GLASS COMPANY, Late 1930s–1960s

	Crystal		Crystal
Bowl, 5", Berry	7.50	Plate, 8", Luncheon	8.50
Bowl, 8½", Large Berry	27.50	Plate, 9¼", Dinner	11.00
Bowl, 10½", Fruit	12.50	Plate, 12", Sandwich	12.50
Cup	6.50	Saucer	4.00
Creamer, Footed	21.00	Sugar, Open, Footed	17.50

HEX OPTIC, "HONEYCOMB"
(pink, green)
JEANNETTE GLASS COMPANY, 1928–1932

	Pink or Green		Pink or Green
Bowl, 4¼", Berry, Ruffled	5.00	Plate, 8", Luncheon	5.00
Bowl, 7½", Large Berry	7.00	Platter, 11", Round	12.00
Butter Dish & Cover, Rectangular,		Refrigerator Dish, 4" x 4"	9.50
1 lb. size	67.50	Salt & Pepper, Pr.	25.00
Bucket Reamer	50.00	Saucer	2.00
Creamer, Two Style Handles	5.00	Sugar, Two Styles of Handles	5.00
Cup, Two Style Handles	4.50	Sugar Shaker	130.00
Ice Bucket, Metal Handle	17.50	Sherbet, 5 oz., Footed	4.00
Pitcher, 5", 32 oz., Sunflower		Tumbler, 3¾", 9 oz.	4.50
Motif in Bottom	20.00	Tumbler, 5¾", Footed	8.50
Pitcher, 9", 48 oz., Footed	37.50	Tumbler, 7", Footed	11.00
Plate, 6", Sherbet	2.00	Whiskey, 2", 1 oz.	7.50

HOBNAIL
(crystal, pink)
HOCKING GLASS COMPANY, 1934–1936

	Crystal
Bowl, 5½", Cereal	3.50
Cup	4.00
Creamer, Footed	4.00
Decanter & Stopper, 32 oz.	25.00
Goblet, Water, 10 oz.	6.00
Goblet, Ice Tea, 13 oz.	7.50
Pitcher, Milk, 18 oz.	17.50
Pitcher, 67 oz.	24.00
Plate, 6", Sherbet	2.00

	Crystal
Saucer	2.00
Sherbet	3.00
Sugar, Footed	4.00
Tumbler, Juice, 5 oz.	4.00
Tumbler, Water, 9 oz., 10 oz.	5.00
Tumbler, Ice Tea, 15 oz.	7.00
Tumbler, Footed Wine, 3 oz.	6.50
Tumbler, Footed Cordial, 5 oz.	6.00
Whiskey, 1½ oz.	6.00

HOLIDAY, "BUTTON AND BOWS"
(pink, iridescent)
JEANNETTE GLASS COMPANY, 1947–1949

	Pink		Pink
Bowl, 5⅛", Berry	11.00	Plate, 6", Sherbet	4.50
Bowl, 7¾", Soup	40.00	Plate, 9", Dinner	15.00
Bowl, 8½", Large Berry	22.00	Plate, 13¾", Chop	85.00
Bowl, 9½", Oval Vegetable	22.00	Platter, 11⅜", Oval	17.50
Bowl, 10¾", Console	87.50	Sandwich Tray, 10½"	15.00
Butter Dish & Cover	35.00	Saucer, Two Style	4.50
Cake Plate, 10½", Three-Legged	80.00	Sherbet	6.00
Candlesticks, 3", Pr.	80.00	Sugar	9.00
Creamer, Footed	7.50	Sugar Cover	13.50
Cup, Two Sizes	6.50	Tumbler, 4", 10 oz., Flat	18.50
Pitcher, 4¾", Milk, 16 oz.	55.00	Tumbler, 4", Footed	35.00
Pitcher, 6¾", 52 oz.	30.00	Tumbler, 6", Footed	125.00

HOMESPUN, "FINE RIB"
(pink, crystal)
JEANNETTE GLASS COMPANY, 1939–1940

	Pink
Bowl, 4½", Closed Handles	9.50
Bowl, 5", Cereal	17.50
Bowl, 8¼", Large Berry	15.00
Butter Dish & Cover	55.00
Coaster/Ashtray	6.00
Creamer, Footed	10.00
Cup	10.00
Plate, 6", Sherbet	5.00
Plate, 9¼", Dinner	15.00
Platter, 13", Closed Handles	14.00
Saucer	4.00
Sherbet, Low Flat	15.00
Sugar, Footed	8.50
Tumbler, 4", Water, 9 oz.	16.00

	Pink
Tumbler, 5¼", Ice Tea, 13 oz.	26.00
Tumbler, 4", 5 oz., Footed	6.50
Tumbler, 6¼", 9 oz., Footed	23.00
Tumbler, 6½", 15 oz., Footed	23.00

CHILD'S TEA SET

	Pink
Cup	26.00
Saucer	8.50
Plate	11.00
Teapot	40.00
Teapot Cover	75.00
Set of 14 Pieces	300.00

INDIANA CUSTARD, "FLOWER AND LEAF BAND"
(ivory or custard, early 1930s; white, 1950s)
INDIANA GLASS COMPANY

	Ivory		Ivory
Bowl, 4⅞", Berry	7.50	Plate, 7½", Salad	10.00
Bowl, 5¾", Cereal	18.00	Plate, 8⅞", Luncheon	12.00
Bowl, 7½", Flat Soup	28.00	Plate, 9¾", Dinner	20.00
Bowl, 8¾", Large Berry	26.00	Platter, 11½", Oval	28.00
Bowl, 9½", Oval Vegetable	25.00	Saucer	8.00
Butter Dish & Cover	60.00	Sherbet	85.00
Cup	35.00	Sugar	10.00
Creamer	15.00	Sugar Cover	18.00
Plate, 5¾", Bread & Butter	6.50		

IRIS, "IRIS AND HERRINGBONE"
(crystal, iridescent)
JEANNETTE GLASS COMPANY, 1928–1932; 1950; 1970

	Crystal	Iridescent
Bowl, 4½", Berry,		
Beaded	35.00	8.00
Bowl, 5", Sauce	8.00	22.00
Bowl, 5", Cereal	95.00	----
Bowl, 7½", Soup	135.00	50.00
Bowl, 8", Large Berry,		
Beaded	75.00	20.00
Bowl, 9½", Salad	12.00	11.00
Bowl, 11", Fruit,		
Ruffled	14.00	12.00
Bowl, 11", Fruit,		
Straight	47.50	----
Butter Dish & Cover	45.00	40.00
Candlesticks, Pr.	37.50	40.00
Candy Jar & Cover	97.50	----
Coaster	70.00	----
Creamer, Footed	10.00	11.00
Cup	14.00	12.00
Demitasse Cup	30.00	110.00

	Crystal	Iridescent
Demitasse Saucer	115.00	140.00
Goblet, 4", Wine	----	30.00
Goblet, 4½", Wine	16.00	----
Goblet, 5¾", 4 oz.	22.00	100.00
Goblet, 5¾", 8 oz.	22.00	110.00
Pitcher, 9½", Footed	35.00	35.00
Plate, 5½", Sherbet	12.00	11.00
Plate, 8", Luncheon	60.00	----
Plate, 9", Dinner	47.50	35.00
Plate, 11¾", Sandwich	25.00	25.00
Saucer	10.00	9.00
Sherbet, 2½", Footed	21.00	12.00
Sherbet, 4", Footed	18.00	----
Sugar	10.00	10.00
Sugar Cover	11.00	11.00
Tumbler, 4", Flat	100.00	----
Tumbler, 6", Footed	16.00	15.00
Tumbler, 6½", Footed	30.00	----
Vase, 9"	25.00	22.00

JUBILEE
(topaz, pink)
LANCASTER GLASS COMPANY, Early 1930s

	Topaz		Topaz
Bowl, 9", Fruit, Handled	100.00	Plate, 7", Salad	13.00
Candlesticks, Pr.	150.00	Plate, 8¾", Luncheon	13.00
Cheese & Cracker Set	250.00	Plate, 13", Sandwich	45.00
Creamer	20.00	Saucer	6.00
Cup	14.00	Sherbet, 4¾"	45.00
Goblet, 5", 6 oz.	65.00	Sugar	20.00
Goblet, 6", 10 oz.	37.50	Tray, 11", Cake, Two Handles	40.00
Goblet, 6⅛", 12½ oz.	95.00	Tray, Sandwich, Center Handle	185.00
Mayonnaise, w/Plate & Ladle	245.00		

"LACE EDGE," "OPEN LACE" OLD COLONY
(pink, crystal)
HOCKING GLASS COMPANY, 1935–1938

	Pink		Pink
Bowl, 6⅜", Cereal	16.00	Plate, 7¼", Salad	19.00
Bowl, 7¾", Salad	18.00	Plate, 8¾", Luncheon	15.00
Bowl, 9½", Plain or Ribbed	17.50	Plate, 10½", Dinner	24.00
Bowl, 10½", Three Legs	175.00	Plate, 10½", Grill	16.00
Butter Dish or Bon Bon w/Cover	55.00	Plate, 13", Four-Part Solid Lace	25.00
Candlesticks, Pr.	175.00	Platter, 12¾"	25.00
Candy Jar & Cover, Ribbed	42.50	Platter, 12¾", Five-Part	25.00
Compote, 7"	20.00	Relish Dish, 7½" Deep,	
Compote & Cover, Footed	40.00	Three-Part	55.00
Cookie Jar & Cover	55.00	Saucer	10.00
Creamer	20.00	Sherbet, Footed	75.00
Cup	20.00	Sugar	20.00
Fish Bowl, 1 gal., 80 oz.		Tumbler, 4½", 9 oz., Flat	16.00
(crystal only)	25.00	Tumbler, 5", 10½ oz., Footed	60.00
Flower Bowl, crystal frog	20.00	Vase, 7"	295.00

LACED EDGE, "KATY BLUE"
(blue with opalescent edge; green with opalescent edge)
IMPERIAL GLASS COMPANY, Early 1930s

	Blue or Green		Blue or Green
Bowl, 4½", Fruit	25.00	Plate, 10", Dinner	65.00
Bowl, 7", Soup	60.00	Plate, 12", Luncheon	
Bowl, 9", Vegetable	95.00	(per catalog description)	65.00
Bowl, 11", Divided Oval	95.00	Platter, 13"	125.00
Bowl, 11", Oval	100.00	Saucer	14.00
Cup	30.00	Sugar	32.50
Creamer	32.50	Tidbit, w/8" & 10" Plates	85.00
Mayonnaise, Three-Piece	110.00	Tumbler, 9 oz.	50.00
Plate, 6½", Bread & Butter	18.00	Vase, 5½"	55.00
Plate, 8", Salad	30.00		

LAKE COMO
(white with blue decoration)
ANCHOR HOCKING GLASS COMPANY, 1934–1937

Bowl, 6", Cereal	20.00	Plate, Dinner, 9¼"	25.00
Bowl, Flat Soup	85.00	Platter, 11"	55.00
Bowl, Vegetable, 9¾"	35.00	Salt & Pepper, Pr.	37.50
Creamer, Footed	25.00	Saucer	10.00
Cup	25.00	Sugar, Footed	25.00
Plate, Salad, 7¼"	16.00		

LAUREL
(French ivory, jade green, white opal and poudre blue)
McKEE GLASS COMPANY, 1930s

	Ivory	Green		Ivory	Green
Bowl, 5" Berry	7.00	6.00	Salt & Pepper	45.00	55.00
Bowl, 6", Cereal	9.00	7.00	Saucer	3.00	3.00
Bowl, 6", Three Legs	14.00	13.00	Sherbet	11.00	9.00
Bowl, 9", Large Berry	20.00	16.00	Sugar, Short	9.00	7.50
Bowl, 9¾",			Sugar, Tall	12.00	10.00
Oval Vegetable	16.00	16.00	Tumbler, 4½", 9 oz., Flat	30.00	40.00
Bowl, 10½", Three Legs	33.00	27.00	Tumbler, 5", 12 oz., Flat	40.00	----
Bowl, 11"	35.00	26.00			
Candlesticks, 4", Pr.	27.50	27.50			
Cheese Dish & Cover	55.00	50.00	**CHILDREN'S LAUREL TEA SET**		
Creamer, Short	10.00	9.00			
Creamer, Tall	12.00	11.00	Creamer	20.00	35.00
Cup	7.00	7.00	Cup	15.00	25.00
Plate, 6", Sherbet	5.00	4.00	Plate	7.50	12.50
Plate, 7½", Salad	9.00	9.00	Saucer	5.50	7.50
Plate, 9⅛", Dinner	11.00	11.00	Sugar	20.00	35.00
Plate, 9⅛", Grill	11.00	10.00	14-Piece Set	150.00	250.00
Platter, 10¾", Oval	25.00	18.00			

LINCOLN INN

(amethyst, cobalt, black, red, green, pink, crystal, jade, opaque, green)
FENTON GLASS COMPANY, Late 1920s

	Blue, Red	Other Colors		Blue, Red	Other Colors
Ashtray	16.00	11.00	Goblet, Wine	26.00	16.00
Bon Bon, Handled, Square	14.00	11.00	Nut Dish, Footed	16.00	11.00
Bon Bon, Handled, Oval	15.00	11.00	Pitcher, 7¼", 46 oz.	775.00	675.00
Bowl, 5", Fruit	11.00	9.00	Plate, 6"	7.00	4.00
Bowl, 6", Cereal	12.00	9.00	Plate, 8"	12.00	7.00
Bowl, 6", Crimped	12.00	8.00	Plate, 9¼"	25.00	11.00
Bowl, Handled, Olive	14.00	9.00	Plate, 12"	30.00	15.00
Bowl, Finger	17.00	12.00	Salt & Pepper, Pr	195.00	130.00
Bowl, 9¼", Footed	30.00	18.00	Saucer	4.00	3.00
Bowl, 10½", Footed	40.00	28.00	Sherbet, 4¾"	16.00	11.00
Candy Dish, Footed, Oval	20.00	12.00	Sugar	19.00	13.00
Comport	24.00	14.00	Tumbler, Flat Juice, 4 oz.	25.00	9.00
Creamer	20.00	14.00	Tumbler, 5 oz., Footed	24.00	10.00
Cup	16.00	9.00	Tumbler, 7 oz., Footed	18.00	10.00
Goblet, Water	23.00	15.00	Tumbler, 9 oz., Footed	25.00	13.00
			Tumbler, 12 oz., Footed	38.00	19.00
			Vase, 12", Footed	130.00	85.00

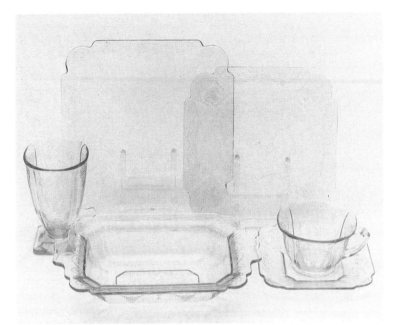

LORAIN, "BASKET," "NO. 615"
(green, yellow, crystal)
INDIANA GLASS COMPANY, 1929–1932

	Green	Yellow		Green	Yellow
Bowl, 6", Cereal	32.50	52.50	Plate, 8⅜", Luncheon	15.00	25.00
Bowl, 7¼", Salad	36.00	54.00	Plate, 10¼", Dinner	35.00	48.00
Bowl, 8", Deep Berry	75.00	125.00	Platter, 11½"	23.00	36.00
Bowl, 9¾", Oval Vegetable	35.00	46.00	Relish, 8", Four-Part	16.00	30.00
Creamer, Footed	15.00	20.00	Saucer	4.00	5.00
Cup	10.00	14.00	Sherbet, Footed	18.00	28.00
Plate, 5½", Sherbet	7.00	10.00	Sugar, Footed	14.00	20.00
Plate, 7¾", Salad	10.00	14.00	Tumbler, 4¾", 9 oz., Footed	18.00	26.00

MADRID
(See Reproduction Section, Page 144–146)
(green, pink, amber, crystal, "Madonna" blue)
FEDERAL GLASS COMPANY, 1932–1939

	Amber	Green		Amber	Green
Ashtray, 6", Square	185.00	130.00	Plate, 6", Sherbet	3.50	4.00
Bowl, 4¾", Cream Soup ...	14.00	----	Plate, 7½", Salad	10.00	9.00
Bowl, 5", Sauce	6.00	6.50	Plate, 8⅞", Luncheon	8.00	8.00
Bowl, 7", Soup	14.00	15.00	Plate, 10½", Dinner	32.50	32.00
Bowl, 8", Salad	14.00	16.00	Plate, 10½", Grill	9.00	15.00
Bowl, 9⅜", Large Berry ...	18.00	----	Plate, 10¼", Relish	12.00	16.00
Bowl, 9½", Deep Salad ...	27.50	----	Plate, 11½", Cake,		
Bowl, 10", Oval Vegetable ..	15.00	16.00	Round	14.00	----
Bowl, 11", Low Console ..	15.00	----	Platter, 11½", Oval	15.00	14.00
Butter Dish & Cover	65.00	75.00	Salt/Pepper, 3½",		
Candlesticks, 2¼", Pr.	20.00	----	Footed	65.00	80.00
Cookie Jar & Cover	42.50	----	Salt/Pepper, 3½", Flat	45.00	62.00
Creamer, Footed	8.00	9.00	Saucer	4.00	4.00
Cup	6.00	8.00	Sherbet, Two Styles	7.50	8.00
Gravy Boat & Platter	1,060.00	----	Sugar	7.00	8.00
Hot Dish Coaster	35.00	35.00	Sugar Cover	35.00	35.00
Hot Dish Coaster			Tumbler, 3⅞", 5 oz.	14.00	30.00
w/Indent	35.00	35.00	Tumbler, 4¼", 9 oz.	14.00	21.00
Jam Dish, 7"	20.00	16.00	Tumbler, 5½", 12 oz.,		
Jello Mold, 2⅛" High	12.00	----	Two Styles	18.00	28.00
Pitcher, 5½", Juice, 36 oz. ..	35.00	----	Tumbler, 4", 5 oz., Footed	23.00	35.00
Pitcher, 8", Square, 60 oz.	45.00	135.00	Tumbler, 5½", 10 oz.,		
Pitcher, 8½", 8 oz.	60.00	200.00	Footed	23.00	32.00
Pitcher, 8½", 80 oz.,			Wooden Lazy Susan,		
Ice Lip	60.00	225.00	7 Hot Dish Coasters	650.00	----

MANHATTAN, "HORIZONTAL RIBBED"
(pink, crystal, green)
ANCHOR HOCKING GLASS COMPANY, 1939–1941

	Crystal	Pink		Crystal	Pink
Ashtray, 4", Round	10.00	----	Relish Tray, 14", Four-Part	16.00	----
Ashtray, 4½", Square	18.00	----	Relish Tray, 14", Five-Part	13.00	15.00
Bowl, 4½", Sauce	9.00	----	Relish Tray Insert	5.00	6.00
Bowl, 5⅜", Berry w/Handles	15.00	15.00	Pitcher, 24 oz.	25.00	----
Bowl, 7½", Large Berry	13.00	----	Pitcher, 80 oz., Tilted	30.00	45.00
Bowl, 8", Closed Handles	20.00	20.00	Plate, 6", Sherbet	5.00	45.00
Bowl, 9", Salad	18.00	----	Plate, 8½", Salad	13.00	----
Bowl, 9½", Fruit (Open Handle)	32.00	30.00	Plate, 10¼", Dinner	17.50	100.00
Candlesticks, 4½" (Square) Pr.	13.00	----	Plate, 14", Sandwich	20.00	----
Candy Dish, Three Legs	----	10.00	Salt/Pepper, 2" (Square), Pr.	25.00	40.00
Candy Dish & Lid	36.00	----	Saucer (Same as 6" Plate)	5.00	45.00
Coaster, 3½"	14.00	----	Sherbet	8.00	12.00
Compote, 5¾"	27.50	27.50	Sugar, Oval	10.00	10.00
Creamer, Oval	10.00	10.00	Tumbler, 10 oz., Footed	15.00	15.00
Cup	16.00	135.00	Vase, 8"	16.00	----
			Wine, 3½"	5.00	----

MAYFAIR, "OPEN ROSE"
(See Reproduction Section, Page 147–149)
(pink, green, blue, yellow, crystal)
HOCKING GLASS COMPANY, 1931–1937

	Pink	Blue		Pink	Blue
Bowl, 5", Cream Soup .	38.00	----	Cup	16.00	45.00
Bowl, 5½", Cereal	20.00	42.00	Decanter & Stopper,		
Bowl, 7", Vegetable	22.00	45.00	32 oz.	130.00	----
Bowl, 9", 3⅛" High,			Goblet, 4" Cocktail,		
Three Leg Console ...	3,750.00	----	3½ oz.	65.00	----
Bowl, 9½", Oval			Goblet, 4½", Wine,		
Vegetable.................	25.00	60.00	3 oz.	65.00	----
Bowl, 10", Vegetable	22.50	60.00	Goblet, 5¾", Water,		
Bowl, 10", Same			9 oz	50.00	----
Covered....................	90.00	100.00	Goblet, 7¼", Thin,		
Bowl, 11¾", Low Flat ...	48.00	60.00	9 oz.	135.00	155.00
Bowl, 12", Deep			Pitcher, 6", 37 oz.	47.50	125.00
Scalloped Fruit.........	48.00	75.00	Pitcher, 8", 60 oz.	45.00	150.00
Butter Dish & Cover or			Pitcher, 8½", 80 oz.	90.00	165.00
7" Covered			Plate, 5¾" (often substituted		
Vegetable	55.00	265.00	as saucer)	12.00	20.00
Cake Plate, Footed	25.00	55.00	Plate, 6½", Round		
Candy Dish & Cover ...	47.50	250.00	Sherbet....................	12.00	----
Celery Dish, 10"	35.00	45.00	Plate, 6½", Round, Off		
Celery Dish, 10",			Center Indent..........	22.50	25.00
Divided	175.00	50.00	Plate, 8½", Luncheon ..	22.00	40.00
Cookie Jar & Lid	45.00	250.00	Plate, 9½", Dinner	45.00	65.00
Creamer, Footed	22.50	60.00	Plate, 9½", Grill	35.00	45.00

	Pink	Blue		Pink	Blue
Plate, 12", Cake w/Handles	35.00	55.00	Sugar Lid	1,400.00	----
Platter, 12", Oval, Open Handles	24.00	55.00	Tumbler, 3½", Juice, 5 oz.	38.00	97.50
Relish, 8⅜", Four-Part or Non-Partitioned	28.00	55.00	Tumbler, 4¼", Water, 9 oz.	25.00	85.00
Salt & Pepper, Flat, Pr.	55.00	265.00	Tumbler, 4¾", Water, 11 oz.	130.00	100.00
Salt & Pepper, Footed, Pr.	5,000.00	----	Tumbler, 5¼", 13½ oz., Ice Tea	40.00	150.00
Sandwich Server/ Center Handle	40.00	65.00	Tumbler, 3¼", Juice, 3 oz., Footed	70.00	----
Saucer (Cup Ring)	27.50	----	Tumbler, 5¼", 10 oz., Footed	32.00	110.00
Saucer (See 5¾" Plate)			Tumbler, 6½", Ice Tea, 15 oz., Footed	32.00	150.00
Sherbet, 2¼", Flat	150.00	95.00	Vase (Sweet Pea)	125.00	95.00
Sherbet, 3", Footed	15.00	----	Whiskey, 2¼", 1½ oz.	60.00	----
Sherbet, 4¾", Footed	75.00	65.00			
Sugar, Footed	25.00	70.00			

MAYFAIR FEDERAL
(crystal, amber, green)
FEDERAL GLASS COMPANY, 1934

	Amber	Green		Amber	Green
Bowl, 5", Sauce	8.00	11.00	Plate, 6¾", Salad	7.00	8.00
Bowl, 5", Cream Soup	17.50	18.00	Plate, 9½", Dinner	12.00	12.00
Bowl, 6", Cereal	17.00	19.00	Plate, 9½", Grill	13.00	13.00
Bowl, 10",			Platter, 12", Oval	25.00	28.00
Oval Vegetable	25.00	25.00	Saucer	4.00	4.00
Creamer, Footed	12.50	15.00	Sugar, Footed	12.50	15.00
Cup	8.00	8.00	Tumbler, 4½", 9 oz.	22.50	26.00

MISS AMERICA
(See Reproduction Section, Page 150)
(pink, green, crystal, red)
HOCKING GLASS COMPANY, 1933–1937

	Crystal	Pink
Bowl, 6¼", Berry	9.00	19.00
Bowl, 8", Curved in at top	35.00	65.00
Bowl, 8¾", Straight, Deep Fruit	30.00	50.00
Bowl, 10", Oval Vegetable	14.00	25.00
Butter Dish & Cover	200.00	500.00
Cake Plate, 12", Footed	25.00	40.00
Candy Jar & Cover, 11½"	55.00	125.00
Celery Dish, 10½", Oblong	15.00	25.00
Coaster, 5¾"	15.00	25.00
Compote, 5"	13.00	22.00
Creamer, Footed	9.50	15.00
Cup	9.50	20.00
Goblet, 3¾", Wine, 3 oz.	18.00	60.00
Goblet, 4¾", Juice, 5 oz.	24.00	70.00
Goblet, 5½", Water, 10 oz.	20.00	38.00
Pitcher, 8", 65 oz.	45.00	110.00
Pitcher, 8½", 65 oz., w/Ice Lip	65.00	120.00

	Crystal	Pink
Plate, 5¾", Sherbet	6.00	8.00
Plate, 8½", Salad	7.00	20.00
Plate, 10½", Dinner	12.00	22.00
Plate, 10¼", Grill	10.00	20.00
Platter, 12", Oval	14.00	22.00
Relish, 8¾", Four-Part	9.00	20.00
Relish, 11¾", Round, Divided	22.50	750.00
Salt & Pepper, Pr.	28.00	50.00
Saucer	4.00	6.00
Sherbet	7.50	13.00
Sugar	8.00	15.00
Tumbler, 4", Juice, 5 oz.	16.00	40.00
Tumbler, 4½", Water, 10 oz.	14.00	25.00
Tumbler, 5¾", Ice Tea, 14 oz.	24.00	65.00

MODERNTONE, "WEDDING BAND"
(blue, amethyst, platonite fired-on colors)
HAZEL ATLAS GLASS COMPANY, 1934–1942

	Cobalt	Amethyst
Ashtray, 7¾", Match Holder in Center	115.00	----
Bowl, 4¾", Cream Soup	19.00	16.00
Bowl, 5", Berry	20.00	20.00
Bowl, 5", Cream Soup, Ruffled	40.00	25.00
Bowl, 6½", Cereal	65.00	65.00
Bowl, 7½", Soup	90.00	85.00
Bowl, 8¾", Large Berry	50.00	35.00
Butter Dish w/Metal Cover	95.00	----
Cheese Dish, 7" w/Metal Lid	400.00	----
Creamer	10.00	9.00
Cup	10.00	9.00
Cup (no handle), Custard	18.00	12.00
Plate, 5¾", Sherbet	6.00	5.00
Plate, 6¾", Salad	10.00	9.00
Plate, 7¾", Luncheon	12.00	9.00
Plate, 8⅞", Dinner	16.00	11.00
Plate, 10½", Sandwich	45.00	35.00
Platter, 11", Oval	35.00	28.00
Platter, 12", Oval	55.00	35.00
Salt & Pepper, Pr.	40.00	32.00
Saucer	5.00	4.00
Sherbet	12.00	10.00
Sugar	10.00	9.00
Sugar Lid in Metal	35.00	----
Tumbler, 5 oz.	35.00	25.00
Tumbler, 9 oz.	30.00	22.00
Tumbler, 12 oz.	85.00	75.00
Whiskey, 1½ oz.	30.00	----

MOONDROPS

(amber, pink, green, cobalt blue, ice blue, red, amethyst, crystal, dark green, light green, jadite, smoke, black)
NEW MARTINSVILLE, 1932–1940s

	Red, Blue	Others		Red, Blue	Others
Ashtray	30.00	16.00	Bowl, 13", Console w/"Wings"	110.00	40.00
Bowl, 5¼", Berry	12.00	6.00	Butter Dish & Cover	450.00	250.00
Bowl, 6¾", Soup	70.00	----	Candles, 2", Ruffled, Pr.	35.00	23.00
Bowl, 7½", Pickle	22.00	14.00	Candles, 4½", Sherbet Style, Pr.	26.00	19.00
Bowl, 8⅜", Footed, Concave Top	32.00	20.00	Candlesticks, 5" "Wings," Pr.	85.00	45.00
Bowl, 8½", Three-Footed, Divided Relish	28.00	17.00	Candlesticks, 5¼", Triple Light, Pr.	92.00	50.00
Bowl, 9½", Three-Legged, Ruffled	40.00	23.00	Candlesticks, 8½", Metal Stem, Pr.	37.50	27.50
Bowl, 9¾", Oval Vegetable	30.00	22.00	Candy Dish, 8", Ruffled	35.00	19.00
Bowl, 9¾", Covered Casserole	135.00	95.00	Cocktail Shaker with or w/o Handle, Metal Top	58.00	32.00
Bowl, 9¾", Two Handled, Oval	50.00	35.00	Compote, 4"	20.00	15.00
Bowl, 11½", Celery, Boat Shaped	30.00	23.00	Compote, 11½"	55.00	30.00
			Creamer, 2¾", Miniature	17.50	11.00
Bowl, 12", Three-Footed, Round Casserole	80.00	30.00	Creamer, 3¾", Regular	15.00	9.00
			Cup	15.00	9.00

	Red, Blue	Others
Decanter, Small, 7¾"	65.00	37.50
Decanter, Medium, 8½"	68.00	42.00
Decanter, Large, 11¼"	95.00	50.00
Decanter, "Rocket," 10¼"	400.00	350.00
Goblet, 2⅞", ¾ oz., Liquor	35.00	25.00
Goblet, 4", Wine, 4 oz.	20.00	12.00
Goblet, 4¼", "Rocket" Wine	55.00	30.00
Goblet, 4¾", 5 oz.	22.50	14.00
Goblet, 5⅛", Wine, Metal Stem	15.00	10.00
Goblet, 5½", Wine, Metal Stem	18.00	10.00
Goblet, 6¼", Water, 9 oz., Metal Stem	22.00	15.00
Mug, 5⅛", 12 oz.	35.00	22.00
Perfume Bottle, "Rocket"	195.00	150.00
Pitcher, Small, 6⅞", 22 oz.	150.00	85.00
Pitcher, Medium, 8⅛", 32 oz.	180.00	110.00
Pitcher, Large w/Lip, 8", 50 oz.	185.00	115.00
Pitcher, Large, No Lip, 8⅛", 53 oz.	185.00	125.00
Plate, 5⅞", Bread & Butter	10.00	8.00
Plate, 6⅛", Sherbet	6.00	4.00
Plate, 6", Round, Off-Center Indent for Sherbet	11.00	9.00

	Red, Blue	Others
Plate, 7⅛", Salad	12.00	9.00
Plate, 8½", Luncheon	14.00	11.00
Plate, 9½", Dinner	22.00	15.00
Plate, 14", Round Sandwich	35.00	16.00
Plate, 14", Two-Handled Sandwich	40.00	22.00
Platter, 12", Oval	30.00	20.00
Saucer	5.00	4.00
Sherbet, 2⅝"	15.00	10.00
Sherbet, 4½"	25.00	15.00
Sugar, 2¾"	14.00	9.00
Sugar, 4"	15.00	9.00
Tumbler, 2¾", Shot, 2 oz.	15.00	9.00
Tumbler, 2¾", Handled Shot, 2 oz.	15.00	10.00
Tumbler, 3¾", Juice, 3 oz., Footed	15.00	10.00
Tumbler, 3⅝", 5 oz.	14.00	9.00
Tumbler, 4⅜", 7 oz.	15.00	9.00
Tumbler, 4⅜", 8 oz.	15.00	10.00
Tumbler, 4⅞", Handled, 9 oz.	27.50	15.00
Tumbler, 4⅞", 9 oz.	18.00	14.00
Tumbler, 5⅛", 12 oz.	26.00	14.00
Tray, 7½" for Miniature Sugar/Creamer	35.00	18.00
Vase, 7¾", Flat, Ruffled Top	55.00	55.00
Vase, 9¼", "Rocket" Style	225.00	125.00

MOONSTONE
(crystal with opalescent hobnails)
ANCHOR HOCKING GLASS COMPANY, 1941–1946

	Opalescent		Opalescent
Bowl, 5½", Berry	15.00	Cup	7.00
Bowl, 5½", Crimped Dessert	8.00	Goblet, 10 oz.	18.00
Bowl, 6½", Crimped, Handled	9.00	Heart Bonbon, One Handle	12.00
Bowl, 7¾", Flat	12.00	Plate, 6¼", Sherbet	6.00
Bowl, 7¾", Divided Relish	10.00	Plate, 8", Luncheon	14.00
Bowl, 9½", Crimped	18.00	Plate, 10", Sandwich	22.50
Bowl, Cloverleaf	12.00	Puff Box & Cover, 4¾", Round	20.00
Candleholder, Pr.	16.00	Saucer (same as Sherbet Plate)	6.00
Candy Jar & Cover, 6"	24.00	Sherbet, Footed	6.00
Cigarette Jar & Cover	20.00	Sugar, Footed	8.00
Creamer	8.00	Vase, 5½", Bud	12.00

MOROCCAN AMETHYST
(amethyst)
HAZEL WARE, DIVISION OF CONTINENTAL CAN, 1960s

	Amethyst		Amethyst
Ashtray, ¾", Triangular	5.00	Goblet, 4¼", 7½ oz., sherbet	7.00
Ashtray, 3¼", Round	5.00	Goblet, 4⅜", 5½ oz., juice	8.50
Ashtray, 6⅝", Triangular	9.00	Goblet, 5½", 9 oz., water	10.00
Ashtray, 8", Square	12.50	Ice Bucket, 6"	27.50
Bowl, 4¾", Fruit, Octagonal	6.00	Plate, 5¾"	4.00
Bow, 5¾", Deep, Square	9.00	Plate, 7¼", Salad	6.00
Bowl, 6", Round	10.00	Plate, 9⅜", Dinner	7.50
Bowl, 7¾", Oval	15.00	Plate, 10" Fan-shaped,	
Bowl, 7¾", Rectangular	13.00	Snack w/cup rest	7.50
Bowl, 7¾", Rectangular,		Plate, 12" Sandwich	
w/metal handle	14.00	w/metal handle	10.00
Bowl, 10¾"	25.00	Saucer	1.00
Candy w/Lid, Short	27.50	Tumbler, 2½", Juice, 4 oz.	7.50
Candy w/Lid, Tall	27.50	Tumbler, 3¼", Old Fashion,	
Chip and dip, 10¾" & 5¾",		8 oz.	12.50
Bowls in metal holder	35.00	Tumbler, Water, 9 oz.	10.00
Cocktail w/stirrer, 6¼",		Tumbler, 4¼", Water,	
16 oz., w/lip	25.00	Crinkled Bottom, 11 oz.	11.00
Cocktail Shaker, w/lid	22.50	Tumbler, 4⅝", Water, 11 oz.	11.00
Cup	5.00	Tumbler, 6½", Ice Tea, 16 oz.	15.00
Goblet, 4", 4½ oz., wine	9.00	Vase, 8½", Ruffled	35.00

MT. PLEASANT, "DOUBLE SHIELD"
(black amethyst, amethyst, cobalt blue, green, pink)
L.E. SMITH COMPANY, 1920s–1934

	Black Amethyst, Cobalt
Bonbon, Rolled up Handles, 7"	22.00
Bowl, 4" Opening Rose	25.00
Bowl, 4", Square Fruit, Footed	17.50
Bowl, 6", Two-Handled, Square	16.00
Bowl, 7", Three-Footed, Rolled Out Edge	20.00
Bowl, 8", Scalloped, Two-Handled	25.00
Bowl, 8", Square, Two-Handled	27.50
Bowl, 9", Scalloped, 1¾" Deep, Footed	28.00
Bowl, 9¼", Square Fruit, Footed	27.50
Bowl, 10", Scalloped Fruit	35.00
Bowl, 10", Two-Handled, Turned Up Edge	32.00
Candlesticks, Single, Pr.	26.00
Candlesticks, Double, Pr.	40.00
Creamer	17.50

	Black Amethyst, Cobalt
Cup (Waffle-like Crystal, $3.50)	
Cup	10.00
Leaf, 8"	15.00
Mayonnaise, 5½", 3-Footed	25.00
Mint, 6", Center Handle	20.00
Plate, 7", Two-Handled, Scalloped	14.00
Plate, 8", Scalloped or Square	14.00
Plate, 8", Two-Handled	16.00
Plate, 8¼" Sq. w/Indent for Cup	15.00
Plate, 9", Grill	10.00
Plate, 10½", Cake, Two-Handled	25.00
Plate, 12", Two-Handled	32.00
Salt & Pepper, Two Styles	40.00
Sandwich Server, Center Handled	35.00
Sherbet	15.00
Sugar	17.50
Vase, 7¼"	30.00

NEW CENTURY, and incorrectly, "LYDIA RAY"
(pink, green, crystal, amethyst, cobalt)
HAZEL ATLAS GLASS COMPANY, 1930–1935

	Green
Ashtray/Coaster, 5⅜"	27.50
Bowl, 4½", Berry	11.00
Bowl, 4¾", Cream Soup	16.00
Bowl, 8", Large Berry	16.00
Bowl, 9", Covered Casserole	52.50
Butter Dish & Cover	55.00
Cup	6.00
Creamer	8.00
Decanter & Stopper	47.50
Goblet, Wine, 2½ oz.	22.00
Goblet, Cocktail, 3¼ oz.	20.00
Pitcher, 7¾", 60 oz., with or without Ice Lip	35.00
Pitcher, 8", 80 oz., with or without Ice Lip	37.50
Plate, 6", Sherbet	3.00
Plate, 7⅛", Breakfast	7.00

	Green
Plate, 8½", Salad	8.00
Plate, 10", Dinner	15.00
Plate, 10", Grill	10.00
Platter, 11", Oval	14.00
Salt & Pepper, Pr.	35.00
Saucer	3.00
Sherbet, 3"	8.50
Sugar	7.50
Sugar Cover	15.00
Tumbler, 3½", 5 oz.	10.00
Tumbler, 4⅛", 9 oz.	14.00
Tumbler, 5", 10 oz.	14.00
Tumbler, 5¼", 12 oz.	22.00
Tumbler, 4", 5 oz., Footed	15.00
Tumbler, 4⅞", 9 oz., Footed	18.00
Whiskey, 2½", 1½ oz.	14.00

NEWPORT, "HAIRPIN"
(cobalt blue, amethyst, "Platonite" white and fired-on colors)
HAZEL ATLAS GLASS COMPANY, 1936–1940

	Cobalt	Amethyst		Cobalt	Amethyst
Bowl, 4¼", Berry	15.00	12.00	Plate, 8½", Luncheon ...	12.00	10.00
Bowl, 4¾",			Plate, 11½",		
Cream Soup	16.00	15.00	Sandwich	35.00	30.00
Bowl, 5¼", Cereal	30.00	25.00	Platter, 11¾", Oval	35.00	28.00
Bowl, 8¼",			Salt & Pepper	45.00	38.00
Large Berry	35.00	30.00	Saucer	5.00	5.00
Cup	10.00	9.00	Sherbet	14.00	11.00
Creamer	15.00	13.00	Sugar	15.00	13.00
Plate, 6", Sherbet	6.00	5.00	Tumbler, 4½", 9 oz. ...	30.00	30.00

NORMANDIE, "BOUQUET AND LATTICE"
(iridescent, amber, pink)
FEDERAL GLASS COMPANY, 1933–1940

	Amber	Pink		Amber	Pink
Bowl, 5", Berry	5.00	6.00	Plate, 11", Grill	13.00	16.00
Bowl, 6½", Cereal	13.00	18.00	Platter, 11¾"	15.00	22.00
bowl, 8½", Large Berry	14.00	20.00	Salt & Pepper, Pr.	45.00	65.00
Bowl, 10", Oval Vegetable	14.00	30.00	Saucer	4.00	4.00
Creamer, Footed	7.00	9.50	Sherbet	6.00	8.00
Cup	7.00	8.00	Sugar	7.00	9.00
Pitcher, 8", 80 oz.	65.00	110.00	Sugar Lid	80.00	150.00
Plate, 6", Sherbet	4.00	4.00	Tumbler, 4", Juice, 5 oz.	18.00	40.00
Plate, 8", Salad	8.00	10.00	Tumbler, 4¼", Water, 9 oz.	14.00	35.00
Plate, 9¼", Luncheon	8.00	12.00	Tumbler, 5", Ice Tea,		
Plate, 11", Dinner	25.00	90.00	12 oz.	22.00	65.00

NO. 610, "PYRAMID"
(green, pink, yellow, crystal) (black and blue, 1974–1975 by Tiara)
INDIANA GLASS COMPANY, 1928–1932

	Pink	Yellow
Bowl, 4¾", Berry	17.00	30.00
Bowl, 8½", Master Berry	27.00	50.00
Bowl, 9½", Oval	27.00	48.00
Bowl, 9½", Pickle	29.00	50.00
Creamer	22.00	30.00
Ice Tub	72.00	185.00
Ice Tub & Lid	----	600.00
Pitcher	210.00	425.00

	Pink	Yellow
Relish Tray, Four-Part, Handled	37.50	55.00
Sugar	22.00	30.00
Tray for Creamer & Sugar	20.00	47.50
Tumbler, 8 oz., Footed	27.50	47.50
Tumbler, 11 oz., Footed	40.00	65.00

NO. 612, "HORSESHOE"
(green, yellow, crystal)
INDIANA GLASS COMPANY, 1930–1933

	Green	Yellow
Bowl, 4½", Berry	19.00	18.00
Bowl, 6½", Cereal	20.00	20.00
Bowl, 7½", Salad	17.50	20.00
Bowl, 8½", Vegetable	19.00	25.00
Bowl, 9½", Large Berry	27.50	30.00
Bowl, 10½", Oval Vegetable	18.00	22.00
Butter Dish & Cover	600.00	----
Candy in Metal Holder, Motif on Lid Only	135.00	----
Creamer, Footed	13.50	14.00
Cup	9.00	10.00
Pitcher, 8½", 64 oz.	220.00	250.00
Plate, 6", sherbet	5.00	6.00

	Green	Yellow
Plate, 8⅜", Salad	8.00	9.00
Plate, 9⅜", Luncheon	11.00	12.00
Plate, 10⅜", Dinner	16.00	18.00
Plate, 10⅜", Grill	52.50	----
Plate, 11¼", Sandwich	14.00	16.00
Platter, 10¾", Oval	20.00	22.00
Relish, Three-Part, Footed	18.00	35.00
Saucer	5.00	5.00
Sherbet	13.00	14.00
Sugar, Open	13.50	14.00
Tumbler, 4¼", 9 oz.	150.00	----
Tumbler, 4¾", 12 oz.	150.00	----
Tumbler, 9 oz., Footed	18.00	17.00
Tumbler, 12 oz., Footed	100.00	125.00

NO. 616, "VERNON"
(green, crystal, yellow)
INDIANA GLASS COMPANY, 1930–1932

	Green	Yellow		Green	Yellow
Creamer, Footed	23.00	22.00	Saucer	5.00	5.00
Cup	14.00	14.00	Sugar, Footed	23.00	22.00
Plate, 8", Luncheon	8.50	8.50	Tumbler, 5", Footed	30.00	30.00
Plate, 11", Sandwich	24.00	24.00			

NO. 618, "PINEAPPLE & FLORAL"
(crystal, amber, fired-on red)
INDIANA GLASS COMPANY, 1932–1937

	Crystal	Amber		Crystal	Amber
Ashtray, 4½"	16.00	----	Plate, 9⅜", Dinner	15.00	14.00
Bowl, 4¾"	22.00	15.00	Plate, 11½", Sandwich	14.00	15.00
Bowl, 6", Cereal	23.00	18.00	Platter, 11",		
Bowl, 7", Salad	1.00	9.00	Closed Handles	14.00	17.00
Bowl, 10",			Platter, Relish, 11½",		
Oval Vegetable	23.00	18.00	Divided	18.00	----
Compote, Diamond			Saucer	5.00	5.00
Shaped	1.00	7.00	Sherbet, Footed	17.50	17.50
Creamer, Diamond			Sugar, Diamond		
Shaped	7.00	10.00	Shaped	7.00	9.00
Cream Soup	18.50	18.00	Tumbler, 4¼", 8 oz.	32.50	----
Cup	10.00	9.00	Tumbler, 5", 12 oz.	37.50	----
Plate, 6", Sherbet	5.00	5.00	Vase, Cone Shaped,		
Plate, 8⅜", Salad	8.00	8.00	Large	37.50	----

NO. 622, "PRETZEL"
(crystal)
INDIANA GLASS COMPANY, 1930s

	Crystal Teal		Crystal Teal
Bowl, 4½", Fruit Cup	4.00	Plate, 6", Tab Handled	3.50
Bowl, 7", Olive, Leaf Shaped	4.50	Plate, 8⅜", Salad	5.00
Bowl, 7½", Soup	10.00	Plate, 9⅜", Dinner	8.00
Bowl, 8½", Two-Handled, Pickle	5.00	Plate, 11½", Sandwich	12.00
Bowl, 9⅜", Berry	15.00	Saucer	1.50
Bowl, 10¼", Celery	1.50	Sugar	5.00
Creamer	5.00	Tumbler, Juice, 5 oz.	20.00
Cup	5.00	Tumbler, Water, 9 oz.	22.00
Pitcher, 39 oz.	150.00	Tumbler, 12 oz.	30.00
Plate, 6", Bread & Butter	2.50		

OLD CAFE
(pink, crystal, ruby red)
HOCKING GLASS COMPANY, 1936–1938; 1940

	Pink	Red		Pink	Red
Bowl, 3¾", Berry	3.00	5.00	Olive Dish, 6", Oblong	5.00	----
Bowl, 5", One or Two			Pitcher, 80 oz.	80.00	----
Handles	4.50	----	Plate, 6", Sherbet	2.00	----
Bowl, 5½", Cereal	6.00	9.00	Plate, 10", Dinner	27.50	----
Bowl, 9",			Saucer	2.50	----
Closed Handles	9.00	13.00	Sherbet, Low Footed	6.00	----
Candy Dish, 8", Low	8.00	10.00	Tumbler, 3", Juice	9.00	7.50
Cup	5.00	7.00	Tumbler, 4", Water	10.00	----
Lamp	16.00	22.00	Vase, 7¼"	12.00	15.00

OLD ENGLISH, "THREADING"
(green, pink, amber)
INDIANA GLASS COMPANY, Late 1920s

	All Colors		All Colors
Bowl, 4", Berry	15.00	Pitcher w/Cover	110.00
Bowl, 9", Footed Fruit	25.00	Plate, Indent for Compote	18.00
Bowl, 9½", Flat	30.00	Sandwich Server, Center Handle	50.00
Candlesticks, 4", Pr.	30.00	Sherbet, Two Styles	18.00
Candy Jar w/Lid, Footed	47.50	Sugar	17.00
Candy & Lid, Flat	45.00	Sugar Cover	32.00
Compote, 3½" Tall, 7" Across	18.00	Tumbler, 4½", Footed	20.00
Creamer	17.00	Tumbler, 5½", Footed	30.00
Fruit Stand, 11", Footed	37.50	Vase, Fan, 7"	45.00
Goblet, 5¾", 8 oz.	30.00	Vase, 12", Footed	50.00
Pitcher	60.00		

OVIDE, incorrectly dubbed "New Century"
(green, white, black)
HAZEL ATLAS GLASS COMPANY, 1930–1935

	Green	Black		Green	Black
Bowl, 4¾", Berry	----	7.00	Plate, 6", Sherbet	1.50	----
Bowl, 5½", Cereal	----	7.00	Plate, 8", Luncheon	2.00	----
Bowl, 8", Large Berry	----	14.00	Salt & Pepper, Pr.	26.00	26.00
Candy Dish & Cover	20.00	40.00	Saucer	2.00	3.00
Cocktail, Fruit, Footed	3.00	4.00	Sherbet	2.00	6.00
Creamer	3.00	6.00	Sugar, Open	3.00	6.00
Cup	3.00	6.00			

OYSTER AND PEARL
(pink, crystal, ruby red, white with fired-on pink or green)
ANCHOR HOCKING GLASS, 1938–1940

	Pink	Red
Bowl, 5¼", Round or Handled	6.50	10.00
Bowl, 5¼", Heart Shaped, One Handled	7.00	----
Bowl, 6½" Deep, Handled	9.00	18.00

	Pink	Red
Bowl, 10½", Fruit, Deep	22.00	45.00
Candleholder, 3½", Pr.	20.00	40.00
Plate, 13½", Sandwich	16.00	37.50
Relish Dish, 10¼", Oblong	8.00	----

"PARROT," SYLVAN
(green, amber, crystal)
FEDERAL GLASS COMPANY, 1931–1932

	Green	Amber		Green	Amber
Bowl, 5", Berry	20.00	15.00	Plate, 10½", Grill, Square	----	22.00
Bowl, 7", Soup	35.00	28.00	Plate, 10¼", Square	45.00	45.00
Bowl, 8", Large Berry ...	68.00	70.00	Platter, 11¼", Oblong...	40.00	55.00
Bowl, 10", Oval Vegetable.................	47.50	55.00	Salt & Pepper, Pr.	200.00	----
Butter Dish & Cover ...	275.00	1,100.00	Saucer	12.00	12.00
Creamer, Footed	32.50	45.00	Sherbet, Footed, Cone	20.00	18.00
Cup	32.50	30.00	Sherbet, 4¼" High	250.00	----
Hot Plate, 5"	650.00	600.00	Sugar	30.00	32.00
Jam Dish, 7"	----	30.00	Sugar Cover	120.00	360.00
Pitcher, 8½", 80 oz. 1	1,300.00	----	Tumbler, 4¼", 10 oz. ...	100.00	97.50
Plate, 5¾", Sherbet.....	30.00	16.00	Tumbler, 5½", 12 oz. ...	120.00	110.00
Plate, 7½", Salad	30.00	----	Tumbler, 5¾", Footed, Heavy......................	110.00	120.00
Plate, 9", Dinner	40.00	32.00			
Plate, 10½", Grill, Round	25.00	----			

PATRICIAN, "SPOKE"
(pink, green, amber, crystal)
FEDERAL GLASS COMPANY, 1933–1937

	Amber	Green
Bowl, 4¾", Cream Soup	14.00	18.00
Bowl, 5", Berry	11.00	10.00
Bowl, 6", Cereal	22.00	23.00
Bowl, 8½", Large Berry	42.00	30.00
Bowl, 10", Oval Vegetable	30.00	30.00
Butter Dish & Cover	80.00	96.00
Cookie Jar & Cover	80.00	400.00
Creamer, Footed	9.00	10.00
Cup	8.00	9.00
Pitcher, 8", 75 oz.	100.00	100.00
Pitcher, 8¼", 75 oz.	125.00	125.00
Plate, 6", Sherbet	9.00	7.00
Plate, 7½", Salad	14.00	13.00
Plate, 9", Luncheon	11.00	10.00
Plate, 10½", Dinner	6.00	30.00
Plate, 10½", Grill	13.00	12.00
Platter, 11½", Oval	30.00	20.00
Salt & Pepper, Pr.	50.00	55.00
Saucer	9.00	8.00
Sherbet	12.00	12.00
Sugar	9.00	8.00
Sugar Cover	48.00	48.00
Tumbler, 4", 5 oz.	28.00	28.00
Tumbler, 4½", 9 oz.	24.00	24.00
Tumbler, 5½", 14 oz.	38.00	38.00
Tumbler, 5½", 8 oz., Footed	42.00	45.00

"PATRICK"
(yellow, pink)
LANCASTER GLASS COMPANY, EARLY 1930s

	Yellow	Pink
Bowl, 9", Fruit, Handled	40.00	165.00
Bowl, 11", Console	75.00	145.00
Candlesticks, Pr.	75.00	145.00
Candy Dish, Three-Footed	75.00	148.00
Cheese & Cracker Set	85.00	165.00
Creamer	35.00	120.00
Cup	35.00	115.00
Goblet, 4", Cocktail	45.00	120.00
Goblet, 4¾", Juice, 6 oz.	45.00	130.00
Goblet, 6", Water, 10 oz.	65.00	135.00
Mayonnaise, Three-Piece	125.00	185.00
Plate, 7", Sherbet	10.00	16.00
Plate, 7½", Salad	18.00	110.00
Plate, 8", Luncheon	25.00	115.00
Saucer	10.00	15.00
Sherbet, 4¾"	40.00	125.00
Sugar	35.00	120.00
Tray, 11", Two-Handled	50.00	135.00
Tray, 11", Center-Handled	50.00	135.00

PETALWARE
(pink, crystal, monax, cremax)
MacBETH-EVANS GLASS COMPANY, 1930–1940

	Pink	Monax		Pink	Monax
Bowl, 4½", Cream Soup ...	10.00	9.00	Plate, 6", Sherbet	2.00	2.00
Bowl, 5¾", Cereal	8.00	6.00	Plate, 8", Salad	5.00	3.00
Bowl, 8¾", Large Berry ...	14.00	15.00	Plate, 9", Dinner	8.50	6.00
Cup	6.00	5.00	Plate, 11", Salver	9.00	7.00
Creamer, Footed	7.00	6.00	Platter, 13", Oval	14.00	12.00
Lamp Shade (Many Sizes)	----	7.50	Saucer	2.00	1.50
Mustard w/Metal Cover in			Sherbet, Low, Footed	6.00	6.50
Cobalt Blue Only........	----	10.00	Sugar, Footed	7.00	6.00

PRIMO, "PANELLED ASTER"
(green, yellow)
U.S. COMPANY, Early 1930s

	Yellow/Green		Yellow/Green
Bowl, 4½"	9.00	Plate, 7½"	7.00
Bowl, 7¾"	18.00	Plate, 10", Dinner	15.00
Cake Plate, 10",		Plate, 10", Grill	9.00
Three-Footed	18.00	Saucer	3.00
Coaster/Ashtray	7.50	Sherbet	9.00
Creamer	10.00	Sugar	10.00
Cup	8.00	Tumbler, 5¾", 9 oz.	15.00

PRINCESS
(green, pink, topaz, apricot, some blue)
HOCKING GLASS COMPANY, 1931–1935

	Pink	Green		Pink	Green
Ashtray, 4½"	82.50	65.00	Plate, 11½", Sandwich, Handled	20.00	11.00
Bowl, 4½", Berry	20.00	21.00	Platter, 12", Closed Handles	20.00	20.00
Bowl, 5", Cereal or Oatmeal	21.00	26.00	Relish, 7½", Divided	25.00	22.00
Bowl, 9", Salad, Octagonal	30.00	35.00	Relish, 7½", Plain	150.00	95.00
Bowl, 9½", Hat Shaped	30.00	35.00	Salt & Pepper, 4½", Pr.	45.00	45.00
Bowl, 10", Oval Vegetable	20.00	24.00	Saucer (Same as Sherbet Plate)	9.00	9.00
Butter Dish & Cover	85.00	85.00	Sherbet, Footed	18.00	18.00
Cake Stand, 10"	25.00	20.00	Sugar	10.00	10.00
Candy Dish & Cover	50.00	50.00	Sugar Cover	18.00	18.00
Coaster	60.00	30.00	Tumbler, 3", Juice, 5 oz.	20.00	24.00
Cookie Jar & Cover	50.00	50.00	Tumbler, 4", Water, 9 oz.	20.00	24.00
Creamer, Oval	13.00	12.00	Tumbler, 5¼", Ice Tea, 13 oz.	22.00	32.00
Cup	10.00	11.00	Tumbler, 4¾", 9 oz., Square Foot	45.00	55.00
Pitcher, 6", 37 oz.	48.00	45.00	Tumbler, 5¼", 10 oz., Footed	20.00	28.00
Pitcher, 7⅜", 24 oz., Footed	450.00	500.00	Tumbler, 6½", 12½ oz., Footed	65.00	75.00
Pitcher, 8", 60 oz.	48.00	48.00	Vase, 8"	30.00	28.00
Plate, 5½", Sherbet	9.00	9.00			
Plate, 8", Salad	12.00	12.00			
Plate, 9", Dinner	20.00	22.00			
Plate, 9", Grill	12.00	12.00			
Plate, 11½", Grill, Closed Handles	7.00	9.00			

QUEEN MARY, "VERTICAL RIBBED"
(pink, crystal)
HOCKING GLASS COMPANY, 1936–1940

	Pink	Crystal
Ashtray, 2" x 3¾", Oval	4.50	3.00
Bowl, 4", One Handle or None	4.50	3.00
Bowl, 5", Berry; 6", Cereal	20.00	6.00
Bowl, 5½", Two Handles	6.00	4.00
Bowl, 8¾", Large Berry	15.00	9.00
Butter Dish or Preserve & Cover	95.00	22.00
Candy Dish & Cover	30.00	18.00
Candlesticks, 4½", Double Branch, Pr.	----	14.00
Celery or Pickle Dish, 5"x 10"	20.00	8.00
Cigarette Jar, Oval, 2" x 3"	7.00	5.00
Coaster, 3½"	3.50	2.50
Coaster/Ashtray, 4¼", Square	5.00	4.50
Compote, 5¾"	12.00	6.00

	Pink	Crystal
Creamer, Oval	7.00	5.00
Cup	7.00	5.00
Plate, 6" & 6⅝"	4.00	3.00
Plate, 8½", Salad	----	5.00
Plate, 9¾", Dinner	35.00	13.00
Plate, 12", Sandwich	13.00	9.00
Plate, 14", Serving Tray	18.00	12.00
Relish Tray, 12", 3-Part	12.00	10.00
Relish Tray, 14", 4-Part	15.00	12.00
Salt & Pepper, Pr.	----	17.50
Saucer	2.00	1.25
Sherbet, Footed	6.00	4.00
Sugar, Oval	7.00	5.00
Tumbler, 3½", Juice, 5 oz.	9.00	4.00
Tumbler, 4", Water, 9 oz.	10.00	5.00
Tumbler, 5", 10 oz., Footed	35.00	25.00

RADIANCE
(red, cobalt and ice blue, amber, crystal)
NEW MARTINSVILLE, 1936–1939

	Red Blue	Other Colors		Red Blue	Other Colors
Bonbon, 6"	15.00	8.00	Creamer	20.00	12.00
Bonbon, 6", Footed	17.50	10.00	Cruet, Individual	47.50	30.00
Bonbon, 6", Covered	45.00	28.00	Cup	16.00	12.00
Bowl, 5", Two-Handled			Decanter, Handled,		
Nut	15.00	8.00	w/Stopper	140.00	80.00
Bowl, 7", Two-Part	18.00	12.00	Lamp, 12"	95.00	55.00
Bowl, 7', Pickle	18.00	12.00	Mayonnaise,		
Bowl, 8", Three-Part			Three-Piece Set	55.00	25.00
Relish	25.00	18.00	Pitcher, 64 oz.	195.00	135.00
Bowl, 10", Celery	20.00	12.00	Plate, 8", Luncheon	15.00	9.00
Bowl, 10", Crimped	35.00	18.00	Plate, 14", Punch Bowl		
Bowl, 10", Flared	35.00	19.00	Liner	65.00	30.00
Bowl, 12", Crimped	40.00	26.00	Punch Bowl	150.00	75.00
Bowl, 12", Flared	37.50	22.00	Punch Cup, Flat	12.00	6.00
Butter Dish	395.00	180.00	Punch Ladle	100.00	75.00
Candlestick, 8", Pr.	55.00	35.00	Salt & Pepper, Pr.	75.00	45.00
Candle, Two-Light, Pr.	85.00	55.00	Saucer	8.00	6.00
Cheese & Cracker, 11"			Sugar	20.00	12.00
Plate Set	45.00	25.00	Tray, Oval	30.00	22.00
Comport, 5"	25.00	15.00	Tumbler, 9 oz.	25.00	16.00
Comport, 6"	30.00	18.00	Vase, 10", Flared	50.00	28.00
Condiment Set, Four-Piece			Vase, 12", Crimped	65.00	40.00
on Tray	250.00	130.00			

RAINDROPS, "OPTIC DESIGN"
(green, crystal)
FEDERAL GLASS COMPANY, 1929–1933

	Green		Green
Bowl, 4½", Fruit	4.50	Salt & Pepper, Pr.	250.00
Bowl, 6", Cereal	7.00	Saucer	1.50
Bowl, 7½", Berry	35.00	Sherbet	6.00
Cup	5.00	Sugar	6.00
Creamer	7.00	Sugar Cover	35.00
Plate, 6", Sherbet	2.50	Tumbler, 3", 4 oz.	4.00
Plate, 8", Luncheon	5.00	Whiskey, 1⅞"	7.00

RIBBON
(green, black, crystal)
HAZEL ATLAS GLASS COMPANY, 1930–1932

	Green	Black		Green	Black
Bowl, 4", Berry	9.00	----	Salt & Pepper, Pr.	25.00	37.50
Bowl, 8", Large Berry	23.00	30.00	Saucer	2.00	----
Candy Dish & Cover	35.00	----	Sherbet, Footed	4.50	----
Creamer, Footed	12.00	----	Sugar, Footed	12.00	----
Cup	4.50	----	Tumbler, 5½", 10 oz.	12.00	----
Plate, 6¼", Sherbet	2.00	----	Tumbler, 6½", 13 oz.	25.00	----
Plate, 8", Luncheon	4.00	12.00			

RING, "BANDED RINGS"
(crystal, green and crystal with decoration)
HOCKING GLASS COMPANY, 1927–1932

	Crystal	Green & Crystal w/dec.		Crystal	Green & Crystal w/dec.
Bowl, 5", Berry	3.50	4.50	Sandwich Server, Center		
Bowl, 7", Soup	8.00	12.00	Handle	15.00	24.00
Bowl, 8", large Berry	6.50	9.00	Saucer	1.50	2.00
Butter Tub or Ice Bucket	16.00	28.00	Sherbet, Low (for 6½"		
Cocktail Shaker	17.50	23.00	Plate)	4.50	11.00
Cup	4.00	5.00	Sherbet, 4¾", Footed	4.50	8.50
Creamer, Footed	4.50	5.50	Sugar, Footed	4.00	5.00
Decanter & Stopper	21.00	32.00	Tumbler, 3½", 5 oz.	3.00	6.00
Goblet, 7" to 8" (varies),			Tumbler, 4¼", 9 oz.	4.00	6.50
9 oz	7.00	14.00	Tumbler, 5⅛", 12 oz.	5.50	8.00
Ice Tub	13.00	20.00	Tumbler, 3½", Footed		
Pitcher, 8", 60 oz.	15.00	19.00	Cocktail	5.50	7.00
Pitcher, 8½", 80 oz.	18.00	28.00	Tumbler, 5½", Water,		
Plate, 6¼", Sherbet	1.50	2.00	Footed	5.00	8.00
Plate, 6½", Off-Center			Tumbler, 6½", ice Tea,		
Ring	2.00	5.00	Footed	6.50	13.00
Plate, 8", Luncheon	2.00	4.00	Vase, 8"	15.00	30.00
* Salt & Pepper, 3", Pr.	16.00	35.00	Whiskey, 2", 1½ oz.	4.00	8.00

* Green - $55.00

ROCK CRYSTAL, "EARLY AMERICAN ROCK CRYSTAL"

(pink, green, cobalt, red, yellow, amber, blue-green, crystal)
McKEE GLASS COMPANY, 1920s and 1930s in color

	Crystal	Red		Crystal	Red
Bonbon, 7½", S.E.	17.50	50.00	Candelabra, Three-Light,		
Bowl, 4", 5", Fruit, S.E.	10.00	30.00	Pr...................................	45.00	250.00
Bowl, 5", Finger Bowl			Candlesticks, 5½", Low,		
w/7" Plate, P.E............	18.00	55.00	Pr...................................	30.00	125.00
Bowl, 7", Pickle or			Candlesticks, 8½", Tall,		
Spoon Tray..................	18.00	55.00	Pr...................................	68.00	325.00
Bowl, 7", 8", Salad, S.E....	18.00	60.00	Candy & Cover, Round ...	40.00	150.00
Bowl, 9", 10½", Salad,			Cake Stand, 11", Footed,		
S.E.	22.00	90.00	2¾" High	30.00	95.00
Bowl, 11½", Two-Part,			Compote, 7"	30.00	60.00
Relish...........................	28.00	60.00	Creamer, 9 oz., Footed ...	18.00	60.00
Bowl, 12", Oblong Celery ...	23.00	55.00	Cruet & Stopper, Oil,		
Bowl, 12½", Footed			6 oz.............................	75.00	----
Center Bowl.................	48.00	250.00	Cup, 7 oz.	16.00	65.00
Bowl, 13", Roll Tray	28.00	----	Goblet, 7½", 8 oz., Low		
Bowl, 14",			Footed..........................	14.00	50.00
Six-Part Relish	33.00	----	Goblet, 11 oz., Ice Tea,		
Candelabra, Two-Light,			Low Footed.................	18.00	60.00
Pr...................................	38.00	185.00	Jelly, 5", Footed, S.E.	16.00	45.00

S.E. - McKee designation for scalloped edge
P.E. - McKee designation for plain edge

	Crystal	Red
Lamp, Electric	150.00	600.00
Parfait, 3½ oz., Low Foot	16.00	65.00
Pitcher, ½ Gal., 7½" High	85.00	----
Pitcher, Large	150.00	500.00
Plate, 6", Bread & Butter, S.E.	5.00	15.00
Plate, 7½", 8½", Salad, P.E. & S.E.	7.50	20.00
Plate, 9", 10½", 11½", Cake, S.E. (small center design)	15.00	50.00
Plate, 10½", Dinner, S.E. (large center design)	45.00	150.00
Salt & Pepper, Two Styles	68.00	----
Salt Dip	35.00	----
Sandwich Server, Center Handled	25.00	125.00
Saucer	7.00	20.00
Sherbet or Egg, 3½ oz., Footed	16.00	55.00
Stemware, 1 oz., Footed Cordial	27.50	55.00
Stemware, 2 oz., 3 oz., Footed Wines	17.00	45.00
Stemware, 3½ oz., Footed Cocktail	14.00	38.00
Stemware, 6 oz., Footed Champagne	15.00	30.00
Stemware, 8 oz., Large Footed Goblet	16.00	50.00
Sundae, 6 oz., Low Footed	11.00	32.00
Sugar, 10 oz., Open, Flat	17.50	----
Sugar, 10 oz., Covered, Footed	35.00	95.00
Tumbler, Whiskey, 2½ oz.	15.00	50.00
Tumbler, Juice, 5 oz.	14.00	50.00
Tumbler, Old Fashioned, 5 oz.	15.00	50.00
Tumbler, 9 oz., Concave or Straight	18.00	45.00
Tumbler, 12 oz., Concave or Straight	23.00	60.00
Vase, 11", Footed	45.00	150.00

S.E. - McKee designation for scalloped edge
P.E. - McKee designation for plain edge

ROSE CAMEO
(green)
BELMONT TUMBLER COMPANY, 1931

	Green		Green
Bowl, 4½", Berry	8.00	Plate, 7", Salad	9.00
Bowl, 5", Cereal	12.00	Sherbet	10.00
Bowl, 6", Straight Side	16.00	Tumbler, 5", Footed, Two Styles	16.00

ROSEMARY, "DUTCH ROSE"
(pink, green, amber)
FEDERAL GLASS COMPANY 1935–1937

	Amber	Green		Amber	Green
Bowl, 5", Berry	5.00	8.00	Plate, 6¾", Salad	5.00	8.00
Bowl, 5", Cream Soup	14.00	18.00	Plate, Dinner	8.50	12.00
Bowl, 6", Cereal	25.00	28.00	Plate, Grill	7.00	12.00
Bowl, 10", Oval Vegetable	13.00	25.00	Platter, 12", Oval	14.00	18.00
Creamer, Footed	8.00	12.00	Saucer	4.00	5.00
Cup	5.00	9.00	Sugar, Footed	8.00	12.00
			Tumbler, 4¼", 9 oz.	26.00	28.00

ROXANA
(yellow, white, crystal)
HAZEL ATLAS GLASS COMPANY, 1932

	Yellow		Yellow
Bowl, 4½" x 2⅜"	9.00	Plate, 6"	6.00
Bowl, 5", Berry	8.00	Sherbet, Footed	8.00
Bowl, 6", Cereal	12.00	Tumbler, 4", 9 oz.	15.00
Plate, 5½"	7.00		

ROYAL LACE
(pink, green, crystal, blue)
HAZEL ATLAS GLASS COMPANY, 1934–1941

	Pink	Blue		Pink	Blue
Bowl, 4¾", Cream Soup...	18.00	33.00	Nut Dish	350.00	750.00
Bowl, 5", Berry	24.00	45.00	Pitcher, 48 oz., Straight		
Bowl, 10", Round Berry ...	25.00	55.00	Sides	60.00	115.00
Bowl, 10", Three-Leg,			Pitcher, 8", 68 oz.	70.00	200.00
Straight Edge	30.00	55.00	Pitcher, 8", 86 oz.	75.00	200.00
Bowl, 10", Three-Leg,			Pitcher, 8½", 96 oz.	80.00	225.00
Rolled Edge	40.00	275.00	Plate, 6", Sherbet	7.00	15.00
Bowl, 10", Three-Leg,			Plate, 8½", Luncheon	16.00	35.00
Ruffled Edge	38.00	400.00	Plate, 10", Dinner	18.00	38.00
Bowl, 11", Oval			Plate, 9⅞", Grill	14.00	38.00
Vegetable	28.00	50.00	Platter, 13", Oval	28.00	55.00
Butter Dish & Cover	135.00	525.00	Salt & Pepper, Pr.	55.00	230.00
Candlesticks, Straight			Saucer	6.00	10.00
Edge, Pr.	38.00	95.00	Sherbet, Footed	15.00	42.00
Candlesticks, Rolled			Sugar	12.00	35.00
Edge, Pr.	45.00	175.00	Sugar Lid	35.00	140.00
Candlesticks, Ruffled			Tumbler, 3½", 5 oz.	22.00	45.00
Edge, Pr.	45.00	185.00	Tumbler, 4⅛", 9 oz.	15.00	36.00
Cookie Jar & Cover	45.00	300.00	Tumbler, 4⅞", 10 oz.	50.00	95.00
Creamer, Footed	16.00	50.00	Tumbler, 5⅜", 12 oz.	45.00	70.00
Cup	12.00	32.50			

ROYAL RUBY
(red)
ANCHOR HOCKING GLASS COMPANY, 1939–1960s

	Red		Red
Ashtray, 4½", Square	3.00	Plate, 7¾", Luncheon	6.00
Bowl, 4¼", Berry	5.00	Plate, 9" or 9¼", Dinner	10.00
Bowl, 5¼"	12.00	Plate, 13¾"	22.50
Bowl, 7½", Soup	12.00	Punch Bowl & Stand	67.50
Bowl, 8", Oval Vegetable	35.00	Punch Cup	2.50
Bowl, 8½", Large Berry	16.00	Saucer (Round or Square)	2.50
Bowl, 10", Deep	36.00	Sherbet, Footed	8.00
Bowl, 11½", Salad	30.00	Sugar, Flat	7.00
Card Holder	50.00	Sugar, Footed	8.00
Creamer, Flat	7.00	Sugar Lid	9.00
Creamer, Footed	8.50	Tumbler, 2½", Footed Wine	12.50
Cup (Round or Square)	4.50	Tumbler, 3½", Cocktail	9.50
Goblet, Ball Stem	9.00	Tumbler, 5 oz., Juice, Two Styles	5.00
Lamp	35.00	Tumbler, 9 oz., Water	6.00
Pitcher, 22 oz., Tilted or Upright	25.00	Tumbler, 13 oz., Ice Tea	14.00
Pitcher, 3 Qt., Tilted	35.00	Vase, 4", Ball-Shaped	4.50
Pitcher, 3 Qt., Upright	45.00	Vase, 6½", Bulbous, Tall	7.50
Plate, 6½", Sherbet	3.00	Vases, Several Styles (small)	5.00
Plate, 7", Salad	5.00	Vases, Several Styles (large)	10.00

"S" PATTERN, "STIPPLED ROSE BAND"
(crystal, amber)
MacBETH-EVANS GLASS COMPANY, 1930-1933

	Crystal	Amber		Crystal	Amber
Bowl, 5½", Cereal	3.50	4.50	Plate, 11", Heavy Cake	35.00	38.00
Bowl, 8½", Large Berry	8.50	14.00	Plate, 13", Heavy Cake	55.00	63.00
Creamer, Thick or Thin	5.00	6.00	Saucer	1.50	2.00
Cup, Thick or Thin	3.00	4.00	Sherbet, Low Footed	4.00	7.00
Pitcher, 80 oz.	45.00	90.00	Sugar, Thick & Thin	5.00	6.00
Plate, 6", Sherbet	2.00	2.50	Tumbler, 3½", 5 oz.	4.00	6.00
Plate, 8", Luncheon	4.00	4.50	Tumbler, 4", 9 oz.	4.50	6.50
Plate, 9¼", Dinner	5.00	7.00	Tumbler, 4¼", 10 oz.	4.50	7.00
Plate, Grill	6.00	8.00	Tumbler, 5", 12 oz.	8.50	12.00

SANDWICH

(See Reproduction Section, Page 152)
(crystal, 1930–1960s; amber [desert gold], 1960s; pink and ruby red, 1939–1940; forest green, 1950–1960s; white [opaque], 1950s)
HOCKING GLASS COMPANY, 1939–1964

	Crystal	Green		Crystal	Green
Bowl, 4⅞", Berry	5.00	3.00	Pitcher, 6", Juice	50.00	115.00
Bowl, 6", Cereal	26.00	----	Pitcher, ½ gal., Ice Lip	65.00	275.00
Bowl, 6½", Smooth or			Plate, 7", Dessert	9.00	----
Scalloped	7.00	35.00	Plate, 8"	3.50	----
Bowl, 7", Salad	7.00	50.00	Plate, 9", Dinner	16.00	65.00
Bowl, 8", Smooth or			Plate, 9" Indent for		
Scalloped	7.50	60.00	Punch Cup	4.50	----
Bowl, 8¼", Oval	7.50	----	Plate, 12", Sandwich	20.00	----
Butter Dish, Low	40.00	----	Saucer	1.00	11.00
Cookie Jar & Cover	35.00	----	Sherbet, Footed	7.00	----
Creamer	5.00	22.00	Sugar & Cover	20.00	22.00*
Cup, Tea or Coffee	2.00	18.00	Tumbler, 5 oz., Juice	6.00	3.50
Custard Cup	3.50	1.50	Tumbler, 9 oz., Water	7.50	4.50
Custard Cup Liner	13.00	1.50	Tumbler, 9 oz., Footed	21.00	----

* No Lid

SANDWICH

(See Reproduction Section, Page 153)
(crystal, amber, pink, red, teal blue, light green)
INDIANA GLASS COMPANY, 1920–1970s

	Crystal	Pink		Crystal	Pink
Ashtray Set (Club, Spade, Heart, Diamond Shapes) each	3.00	----	Pitcher, 68 oz.	20.00	----
			Plate, 6", Sherbet	2.00	----
			Plate, 7", Bread & Butter ...	3.00	----
Bowl, 4¼", Berry	3.50	----	Plate, 8", Oval, Indent for Sherbet	5.00	----
Bowl, 6"	3.50	----			
Bowl, 6", Six Sides	4.50	----	Plate, 8⅜", Luncheon	4.00	----
Bowl, 8¼"	10.00	----	Plate, 10½", Dinner	8.00	12.00
Bowl, 9", Console	15.00	15.00	Plate, 13", Sandwich	10.00	10.00
Bowl, 11½", Console	15.00	----	Sandwich Server, Center Handle	18.00	25.00
Butter Dish & Cover, Domed	20.00	----			
			Saucer	2.00	----
Candlesticks, 3½", Pr.	15.00	13.00	Sugar	8.50	----
Candlesticks, 7", Pr.	25.00	----	Tumbler, 3 oz., Footed Cocktail	7.00	----
Creamer	8.50	----			
Cruet, 6½" & Stopper	25.00	----	Tumbler, 8 oz., Footed Water	8.00	----
Cup	3.00	----			
Creamer & Sugar on Diamond-Shaped Tray	15.00	----	Tumbler, 12 oz., Footed Ice Tea	10.00	----
Decanter & Stopper	20.00	85.00	Wine, 3", 4 oz.	6.00	----
Goblet, 9 oz.	12.50	----			

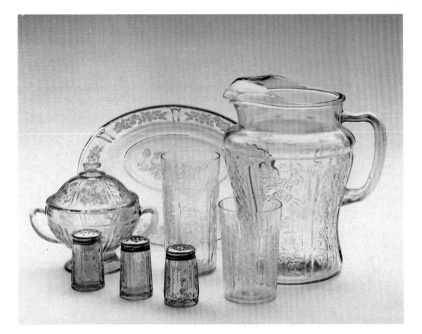

SHARON, "CABBAGE ROSE"
(See Reproduction Section, Page 154–156)
(pink, green, amber, crystal)
FEDERAL GLASS COMPANY, 1935–1939

	Amber	Pink		Amber	Pink
Bowl, 5", Berry	7.50	10.00	Plate, 6", Bread & Butter	4.00	6.00
Bowl, 5", Cream Soup	25.00	36.00	Plate, 7½", Salad	15.00	20.00
Bowl, 6", Cereal	18.00	20.00	Plate, 9½", Dinner	10.00	16.00
Bowl, 7½", Flat Soup,			Platter, 12½", Oval	18.00	25.00
2" Deep	40.00	38.00	Salt & Pepper, Pr.	38.00	45.00
Bowl, 8½", Large Berry	6.00	25.00	Saucer	6.00	9.00
Bowl, 9½", Oval			Sherbet, Footed	12.00	13.00
Vegetable	20.00	25.00	Sugar	8.00	12.00
Bowl, 10½", Fruit	20.00	32.00	Sugar Lid	20.00	24.00
Butter Dish & Cover	43.00	45.00	Tumbler, 4⅛", 9 oz.,		
Cake Plate, Footed,			Thin	23.00	30.00
11½"	20.00	32.00	Thick	25.00	37.50
Candy Jar & Cover	40.00	45.00	Tumbler, 5¼", 12 oz.,		
Cheese Dish & Cover	175.00	750.00	Thin	45.00	38.00
Creamer, Footed	12.00	16.00	Thick	50.00	70.00
Cup	9.00	12.00	Tumbler, 6½", Footed,		
Jam Dish, 7½"	32.00	150.00	15 oz.	95.00	40.00
Pitcher, 80 oz., with or					
without Ice Lip	120.00	130.00			

SIERRA, "PINWHEEL"
(pink, green)
JEANNETTE GLASS COMPANY, 1931–1933

	Pink	Green
Bowl, 5½", Cereal	10.00	12.00
Bowl, 8½", Large Berry	25.00	25.00
Bowl, 9½", Oval Vegetable	35.00	85.00
Butter Dish & Cover	55.00	60.00
Creamer	15.00	19.00
Cup	10.00	13.00
Pitcher, 6½", 32 oz.	65.00	95.00
Plate, 9", Dinner	15.00	18.00

	Pink	Green
Platter, 11", Oval	35.00	40.00
Salt & Pepper, Pr.	35.00	35.00
Saucer	5.00	6.00
Serving Tray, Two Handles	13.00	16.00
Sugar	15.00	20.00
Sugar Cover	14.00	14.00
Tumbler, 4½", 9 oz., Footed	40.00	65.00

SPIRAL
(green)
HOCKING GLASS COMPANY, 1928–1930

	Green		Green
Bowl, 4¾", Berry	4.50	Preserve & Cover	30.00
Bowl, 7", Mixing	8.00	Salt & Pepper, Pr.	30.00
Bowl, 8", Large Berry	12.00	Sandwich Server,	
Creamer, Flat or Footed	7.00	Center Handle	21.00
Cup	5.00	Saucer	1.50
Ice or Butter Tub	25.00	Sherbet	3.50
Pitcher, 7⅝", 58 oz.	28.00	Sugar, Flat or Footed	7.00
Plate, 6", Sherbet	2.00	Tumbler, 3", Juice, 5 oz.	4.00
Plate, 8", Luncheon	3.00	Tumbler, 5", Water, 9 oz.	7.00
Platter	22.50	Tumbler, 5⅞", Footed	13.00

STARLIGHT
(pink, white, crystal)
HAZEL ATLAS GLASS COMPANY, 1938–1940

	Crystal	Pink		Crystal	Pink
Bowl, 5½", Cereal	6.00	8.00	Plate, 9", Dinner	6.00	----
Bowl, 8½", Closed Handles	6.00	14.00	Plate, 13", Sandwich	12.00	13.00
Bowl, 11½", Salad	16.00	----	Relish Dish	12.00	----
Plate, 6", Bread & Butter	2.50	----	Salt & Pepper, Pr.	20.00	----
Creamer, Oval	5.00	----	Saucer	1.50	----
Cup	4.00	----	Sherbet	11.00	----
Plate, 8½", Luncheon	3.00	----	Sugar, Oval	5.00	----

STRAWBERRY
(pink, green, iridescent)
U.S. GLASS COMPANY, 1928–1931

	Pink or Green		Pink or Green
Bowl, 4", Berry	8.00	Pickle Dish	12.00
Bowl, 6¼", 2" Deep	60.00	Pitcher, 7¾"	135.00
Bowl, 6½", Deep Salad	16.00	Plate, 6", Sherbet	6.50
Bowl, 7½", Deep Berry	20.00	Plate, 7½", Salad	12.00
Butter Dish & Cover	140.00	Sherbet	7.00
Compote, 5¾"	18.00	Sugar, Small, Open	15.00
Creamer, Small	16.00	Sugar, Large	30.00
Creamer, Large, 4⅝"	30.00	Sugar Cover	45.00
Olive Dish, 5", One Handle	12.00	Tumbler, 3⅝", 9 oz.	27.50

SUNFLOWER
(pink, green, ultramarine)
JEANNETTE GLASS COMPANY, Late 1920s

	Pink	Green
Ashtray, 5", Center Design Only	9.00	12.00
Cake Plate, 10", Three Legs	14.00	14.00
Creamer	15.00	17.00
Cup	10.00	12.00
Plate, 9", Dinner	13.00	15.00
Saucer	6.00	8.00
Sugar	15.00	17.00
Tumbler, 4¾", 8 oz., Footed	22.50	28.00
Trivet, 7", Three Legs, Turned-Up Edge	265.00	285.00

SWIRL, "PETAL SWIRL"
(pink, ultramarine, delphite)
JEANNETTE GLASS COMPANY, 1937–1938

	Pink	Ultramarine		Pink	Ultramarine
Ashtray, 5⅜"	6.00	----	Plate, 7¼"	6.00	11.00
Bowl, 5¼", Cereal	9.00	14.00	Plate, 8", Salad	8.00	13.00
Bowl, 9", Salad	16.00	24.00	Plate, 9¼", Dinner	12.00	15.00
Bowl, 10", Footed, Closed Handles	----	30.00	Plate, 12½", Sandwich	11.00	24.00
Bowl, 10½", Console, Footed	18.00	25.00	Salt & Pepper, Pr.	----	40.00
Butter Dish	175.00	245.00	Saucer	3.00	4.50
Candleholders, Double Branch, Pr.	----	40.00	Sherbet, Low Footed	10.00	16.00
Candy Dish, Open, Three Legs	10.00	16.00	Soup, Tab Handles (Lug)	20.00	25.00
Candy Dish w/Cover	85.00	125.00	Sugar, Footed	7.00	14.00
Coaster, 1" x 3¼"	8.00	12.00	Tumbler, 4", 9 oz.	14.00	25.00
Creamer, Footed	7.00	14.00	Tumbler, 5⅛", 13 oz.	36.00	85.00
Cup	6.00	14.00	Tumbler, 9 oz., Footed	16.00	32.00
Pitcher, 48 oz., Footed	----	1,500.00	Vase, 6½", Footed	15.00	20.00
Plate, 6½", Sherbet	4.00	6.00	Vase, 8½", Footed	----	25.00

TEA ROOM
(green, pink)
INDIANA GLASS COMPANY, 1926–1931

	Green	Pink		Green	Pink
Bowl, Finger	45.00	35.00	Plate, 8¼", Luncheon	32.00	28.00
Bowl, 7½", Banana Split	78.00	75.00	Plate, 10½",		
Bowl, 8½", Celery	30.00	25.00	Two-Handled	45.00	40.00
Bowl, 8¾", Deep Salad	77.50	60.00	Relish, Divided	22.50	18.00
Bowl, 9½",			Salt & Pepper, Pr.	50.00	45.00
Oval Vegetable	60.00	55.00	Saucer	25.00	25.00
Candlestick, Low, Pr.	45.00	40.00	Sherbet, Three Styles	25.00	22.00
Creamer, 4"	25.00	25.00	Sugar, 4"	16.00	15.00
Creamer & Sugar			Sugar, Flat w/Cover	175.00	125.00
on Tray, 3½"	65.00	60.00	Sundae, Footed, Ruffled	85.00	65.00
Cup	45.00	45.00	Tumbler, 8½ oz., Flat	80.00	70.00
Goblet, 9 oz.	70.00	60.00	Tumbler, 6 oz., Footed	32.00	30.00
Ice Bucket	55.00	50.00	Tumbler, 9 oz., Footed	30.00	30.00
Lamp, Electric	45.00	40.00	Tumbler, 11 oz., Footed	40.00	35.00
Mustard, Covered	135.00	120.00	Tumbler, 12 oz., Footed	50.00	45.00
Parfait	60.00	55.00	Vase, 9"	55.00	45.00
Pitcher, 64 oz.	135.00	120.00	Vase, 11", Ruffled Edge		
Plate, 6½", Sherbet	30.00	25.00	or Straight	90.00	80.00

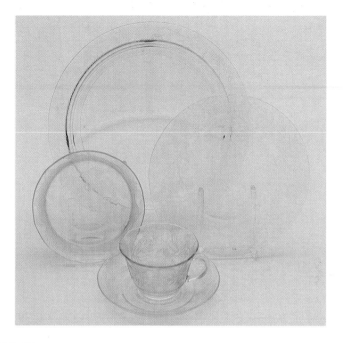

THISTLE
(pink, green)
MacBETH-EVANS, 1929–1930

	Pink	Green		Pink	Green
Bowl, 5½", Cereal	18.00	20.00	Plate, 10¼", Grill	16.00	20.00
Bowl, 10¼", Large Fruit	250.00	160.00	Plate, 13", Cake,		
Cup, Thin	18.00	22.00	Heavy	100.00	125.00
Plate, 8", Luncheon	12.00	16.00	Saucer	9.00	9.00

TWISTED OPTIC
(pink, green, amber, crystal)
IMPERIAL GLASS COMPANY, 1927–1930

	Pink or Green		Pink or Green
Bowl, 4¾", Cream Soup	10.00	Preserve (Same as Candy but w/slot in lid)	25.00
Bowl, 5", Cereal	5.00	Sandwich Server, Center Handle	18.00
Bowl, 7", Salad or Soup	9.00	Sandwich Server, Two-Handled, Flat	10.00
Candlestick, 3", Pr.	17.50	Saucer	1.50
Candy Jar & Cover	25.00	Sherbet	5.50
Creamer	7.00	Sugar	6.00
Cup	3.50	Tumbler, 4½", 9 oz.	6.00
Pitcher, 64 oz.	27.50	Tumbler, 5¼", 12 oz.	8.00
Plate, 6", Sherbet	2.00		
Plate, 7", Salad	2.50		
Plate, 7½" x 9", Oval	5.00		
Plate, 8", Luncheon	3.00		

U.S. SWIRL
(pink, green)
U.S. GLASS COMPANY, Late 1920s

	Green	Pink		Green	Pink
Bowl, 4⅜", Berry	5.00	6.00	Creamer	12.00	14.00
Bowl, 5½", One-Handled	9.00	10.00	Pitcher, 8", 48 oz.	40.00	40.00
Bowl, 7⅛", Large Berry	13.00	15.00	Plate, 6⅛", Sherbet	2.00	2.50
Bowl, 8¼", Oval	23.00	23.00	Plate, 7⅞", Salad	5.00	6.00
Butter & Cover	65.00	70.00	Salt & Pepper, Pr.	40.00	40.00
Butter Bottom	42.50	52.50	Sherbet, 3¼"	4.00	4.50
Butter Top	10.00	15.00	Sugar w/Lid	30.00	35.00
Candy w/Cover,			Tumbler, 4⅝", 12 oz.	10.00	14.00
Two-Handled	25.00	30.00	Vase, 6½"	15.00	18.00

"VICTORY"
(amber, green, pink, cobalt blue)
DIAMOND GLASS-WARE COMPANY, 1929–1932

	Pink	Blue		Pink	Blue
Bonbon, 7"	10.00	19.00	Goblet, 5", 7 oz.	18.00	----
Bowl, 6½", Cereal	10.00	26.00	Gravy Boat & Platter	150.00	290.00
Bowl, 8½", Flat soup	16.00	35.00	Mayonnaise Set: 3½" Tall,		
Bowl, 9", Oval Vegetable	30.00	75.00	5½" Across, 8½" Indented		
Bowl, 11", Rolled Edge	25.00	45.00	Plate w/Ladle	40.00	95.00
Bowl, 12", Console	30.00	----	Plate, 6", Bread & Butter	5.00	15.00
Bowl, 12½", Flat Edge	30.00	60.00	Plate, 7", Salad	6.00	16.00
Candlesticks, 3", Pr.	30.00	85.00	Plate, 8", Luncheon	6.00	25.00
Cheese & Cracker Set,			Plate, 9", Dinner	18.00	35.00
12" Indented			Platter, 12"	25.00	65.00
Plate & Compote	40.00	----	Sandwich Server,		
Comport, 6" Tall, 6¾"			Center Handle	25.00	65.00
Diameter	14.00	----	Saucer	4.00	9.00
Creamer	12.00	40.00	Sherbet, Footed	12.00	25.00
Cup	8.00	30.00	Sugar	12.00	40.00

VITROCK, ("FLOWER RIM")
(white)
ANCHOR HOCKING GLASS COMPANY, 1934–Late 1930s

	White		White
Bowl, 4", Berry	4.00	Plate, 7¼", Salad	2.00
Bowl, 5½", Cream Soup	14.00	Plate, 8¾", Luncheon	4.00
Bowl, 6", Fruit	5.00	Plate, 9", Soup	12.00
Bowl, 7½", Cereal	5.00	Plate, 10", Dinner	8.00
Bowl, Vegetable	10.00	Platter, 11½"	25.00
Creamer, Oval	4.00	Saucer	2.00
Cup	3.00	Sugar, Oval	4.00

WATERFORD, "WAFFLE"
(crystal, pink)
HOCKING GLASS COMPANY, 1938–1944

	Crystal	Pink		Crystal	Pink
Ashtray	6.50	----	Plate, 7⅛", Salad	5.00	7.00
Bowl, 4¾", Berry	6.00	12.00	Plate, 9⅝", Dinner	9.00	16.00
Bowl, 5½", Cereal	16.00	24.00	Plate, 10¼",		
Bowl, 8¼", Large Berry	10.00	15.00	Handled Cake	9.00	14.00
Butter Dish & Cover	24.00	195.00	Plate, 13¾", Sandwich	9.00	24.00
Coaster, 4"	3.00	----	Salt & Pepper, Two Types	8.50	----
Creamer, Oval	5.00	10.00	Saucer	3.00	5.00
Cup	6.00	13.00	Sherbet, Footed	3.50	12.00
Goblet, 5¼", 5⅝"	15.00	----	Sugar	5.00	10.00
Pitcher, Juice, 42 oz.,			Sugar Cover, Oval	5.00	22.00
Tilted	22.00	----	Tumbler, 4⅞", 10 oz.,		
Pitcher, 80 oz., Ice Lip,			Footed	11.00	18.00
Tilted	30.00	130.00	Vase, 6¾"	8.50	----
Plate, 6", Sherbet	2.50	5.00			

WINDSOR, "WINDSOR DIAMOND"
(pink, green, crystal)
JEANNETTE GLASS COMPANY, 1932–1946

	Crystal	Pink		Crystal	Pink
Ashtray, 5¾"	12.50	35.00	Pitcher, 6¾", 52 oz.	12.00	25.00
Bowl, 4¾", Berry	4.00	8.00	Plate, 6", Sherbet	2.00	4.00
Bowl, 5", Cream Soup	5.00	18.00	Plate, 7", Salad	4.00	14.00
Bowl, 5⅛", 5⅜", Cereals	8.00	18.00	Plate, 9", Dinner	5.00	20.00
Bowl, 7⅛", Three Legs	7.00	23.00	Plate, 10¼", Sandwich,		
Bowl, 8½", Large Berry	6.00	15.00	Handled	6.00	15.00
Bowl, 9½",			Plate, 13⅝", Chop	9.00	40.00
Oval Vegetable	6.00	18.00	Platter, 11½", Oval	6.00	18.00
Bowl, 12½",			Relish Platter, 11½",		
Fruit Console	23.00	95.00	Divided	10.00	175.00
Bowl, 7" x 11¾",			Salt & Pepper, Pr.	15.00	35.00
Boat Shape	14.00	30.00	Saucer	2.00	4.50
Butter Dish	25.00	46.00	Sherbet, Footed	3.00	10.00
Cake Plate, 13½" Thick	8.00	18.00	Sugar & Cover	8.00	24.00
Candlesticks, 3", Pr.	16.00	75.00	Tray, 4" Square	5.00	10.00
Candy Jar & Cover	15.00	----	Tray, 4⅛" x 9"	3.50	8.00
Coaster, 3¼"	3.00	10.00	Tray, 8½" x 9¾"	6.50	22.50
Compote	8.00	----	Tumbler, 3¼", 5 oz.	7.50	20.00
Creamer	4.00	10.00	Tumbler, 4", 9 oz.	5.00	16.00
Cup	3.00	9.00	Tumbler, 5", 12 oz.	8.00	25.00
Pitcher, 4½", 16 oz.	19.00	100.00	Tumbler, 7¼", Footed	14.00	----

AUTHOR'S COMMENTS ON REPRODUCTIONS

As popularity of any item in the collecting field grows, there is always someone or some company that will take advantage of the collector. This section will show you the reproductions in Depression Glass through May, 1992.

Know your glassware and your dealer before spending your hard-earned cash for it; also, be wary of deals that seem too good to be true.

The items pictured in this section have all been reproduced since 1973 either by the original glass companies themselves or by private individuals.

Items introduced by companies are usually available in the local dish barns or merchant stores. Those privately manufactured are found at flea markets or local antiques or junk shops.

Some of the glass is marketed through private sales or parties much like the "Tupperware" parties. In these, the buyer is treated to "exclusive lines" of glassware.

My personal feeling is that as long as people buy these reproductions, re-issues, new products made to look old, or what have you, then they will continue to be made either privately or by the companies themselves. I feel also that buying a collectible is an investment; but buying a reproduction is merely speculation. These latter products appeal to me as much as swamp land in Florida.

What can we do? First, we can educate ourselves to know glass; secondly, we can refrain from buying the newer glass. Barring that, we who know the reproductions can label them as such when the opportunity arises.

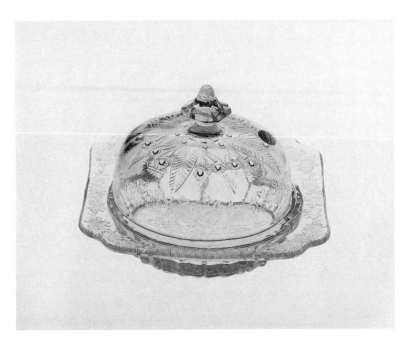

"ADAM"
Privately produced out of Korea through St. Louis Importing Company

The new Adam butter is still being offered at $6.50 wholesale. Identification of the new is easy.

Top: Notice the veins in the leaves.
New: Large leaf veins do not join or touch in center of leaf.
Old: Large leaf veins all touch or join center vein on the old.

A further note in the original Adam butter dish – the veins of all the leaves at the center of the design are very clear-cut and precisely molded, whereas in the new, these center leaf veins are very indistinct and almost invisible in open leaf of the center design.

Bottom: Place butter dish bottom upside down for observation.
New: Four "arrowhead-like" points line up in the northwest, northeast, southeast and southwest directions.
Old: Four "arrowhead-like" points line up in north, east, south and west directions.

There are very bad mold lines and very glossy light pink color on those new butter dishes I have examined but these could be improved.

NEW "AVOCADO"
(pink, frosted pink, yellow, blue, red, amethyst, frost green)
INDIANA GLASS COMPANY, Tiara Exclusives Line, 1974

Thus far, the company has only overlapped the original glass colors in pink and only the pitcher and tumbler sets have been made. The original pink color is lighter in shade than this newer pink which has a slight orange tint.

Some of these sets, such as red, were made in limited editions as a selling point with buyers who are hopeful that someday they may be more valuable. Perhaps they shall, but I personally feel it will take many years for these to have more than their original value.

CHERRY BLOSSOM
(pink, green, blue, delphite, red, cobalt blue, various iridized colors)
PRIVATELY PRODUCED IN 1973...

In 1973 the Depression glass world was stunned with the appearance of a child's butter dish and some odd-looking child's cups – odd because no child's butter dish was made originally and because in the bottoms of the cups, the cherry design was hanging upside-down. Since then, the upside-down design has been rectified and some saucers and plates have appeared. However, all these reproductions are easily spotted. The child's creamer and sugar have not been reproduced!

In 1977 butter dishes and shakers appeared. Some shakers in pink and green were dated '77; other pink, green and delphite shakers appeared non-dated. These shakers are readily recognizable by the almost squared protrusions around the top edge of the shakers. I call them helicopter blades. On the original shakers these protrusions are more rounded and they extend only slightly outward from the top. If you wish to carry your examinations further than that, the design on the shakers is weaker in spots on the newer versions.

The butter dishes pose a bit more problem in distinguishing old from new except in the pretty blue color which wasn't an original color. However, if you use your tactile sense and feel the design inside the butter top, you will find it very sharply defined in the new; also, the knob on the new top is very sharply defined whereas in the old, the knob is more smoothly formed.

Again, about ½" from the edge of the new top, you will notice one ring or band. In the old, there are two distinct indented rings or bands to be noted there.

I could write a book on the differences between old and new scalloped bottom, AOP Cherry pitchers. The easiest way to tell the differences is to turn the pitcher over. My old Cherry Pitcher has nine cherries on the bottom. The new one only has seven. Further, the branch crossing the bottom of my old Cherry pitcher LOOKS like a branch. It's knobby and gnarled and has several leaves and cherry stems directly attached to it. The new pitcher just has a bald strip of glass halving the bottom of the pitcher. Further, the old cherry pitchers have a plain glass background for the cherries and leaves in the bottom of the pitcher. In the new pitchers, there's a rough, filled-in, straw-like background. You see no plain glass (My new Cherry pitcher just cracked sitting in a box by my typing stand — another tendency which I understand is common to the new!)

As for the new tumblers, the easiest way to tell old from the new is to look at the ring dividing the patterned portion of the glass from the plain glass lip. The old tumblers have three indented rings dividing the pattern from the plain glass rim. The new has only one. Further, as in the pitcher, the arching encircling the cherry blossoms on the new tumblers is very sharply ridged. On the old tumblers, that arching is so smooth you can barely feel it. Again, the pattern at the bottom of the new tumblers is brief and practically nonexistent in the center curve of the glass bottom. This was sharply defined on most of the old tumblers. The pattern, what there is, on the new tumblers mostly hugs the center of the foot.

Several different people have gotten into the act of making reproduction Cherry Blossom. We've even enjoyed some reproductions of reproductions! All the items pictured on the next pages are extremely easy to spot as reproductions (colors never made!) once you know what to look for with the possible exception of the 13" divided platter pictured at the back. It's too heavy, weighing 2¾ pounds and has a thick, ⅜" of glass in the bottom; but the design isn't too bad! The edges of the leaves aren't smooth; but neither are they serrated like old leaves.

Now for a quick run-down of the various items.

The Cherry child's dishes were first made in 1973. First to appear was a child's cherry cup with a slightly lop-sided handle and having the cherries hanging upside-down when the cup was held in the right hand. (This defiance of gravity was due to the inversion of the design when the mold, taken from an original cup, was inverted to create the outside of the "new" cup.) After I reported this error, it was quickly corrected by re-inverting the inverted mold. These later cups were thus improved in design but slightly off color. The saucers tended to have slightly off-center designs, too. Next came the "child's butter dish" which was never made by Jeannette. It was essentially the child's cup, without a handle, turned upside-down over the saucer and having a little blob of glass added as a knob for lifting purposes. You could get this item in pink, green, light blue, cobalt, gray-green and iridescent carnival colors. A blue one is pictured on the next page.

Two-Handled Tray - Old: 1⅞ lbs; ³⁄₁₆" glass in bottom; leaves and cherries east/west from north/south handles; leaves have real spine and serrated edges; cherry stems end in triangle of glass.

Two-Handled Tray - New: 2⅛ lbs; ¼" glass in bottom; leaves and cherries north/south with the handles; canal-type leaves (but uneven edges); cherry stem ends before cup-shaped line.

Cake Plate - New: Color too light pink, leaves have too many parallel veins which give them a "feathery" look; arches at plate edge don't line up with lines on inside of the rim to which the feet are attached.

8½" Bowl - New: Crude leaves with smooth edges; veins in parallel lines.

Cereal Bowl - New: Wrong shape, looks like 8½" bowl, 2" center.

Cereal Bowl - Old: Large center, 2½" inside ring, nearly 3½" if you count the outer rim before the sides turn up.

Plate - New: Center has smooth edged leaves, fish spine type center leaf portion; weighs one pound plus; feels thicker at edge with mold offset lines clearly visible on edge.

Plate - Old: Center leaves look like real leaves with spines, veins, and serrated edges; weighs ¾ pound; clean edges; no mold offset on edge.

Cup - New: Area in bottom left free of design; canal leaves; smooth, thick top to cup handle (old has triangle grasp point).

Saucer - New: Off-set mold line edge; canal leaf center.

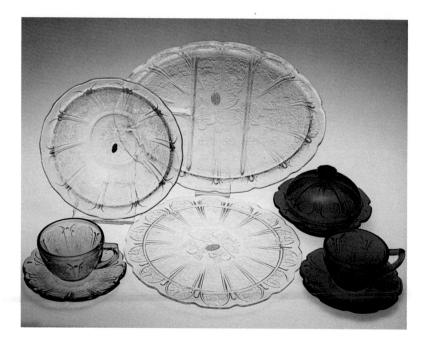

NEW FLORAL
IMPORTING COMPANY OUT OF GEORGIA

The big news in Floral is that *repro-duction shakers* are now being found in pink, red, cobalt blue and a dark green color. Cobalt blue, red, and the dark green Floral shakers are of little concern since they were never made in these colors originally. The green is darker than the original green but not as deep as Forest green. The pink shakers are not only a very good pink, but they are also a very good copy. There are lots of minor variations in design and leaf detail to someone who knows glassware well, but I have always tried to pick out a point that anyone can use to determine validity whether he be a novice or professional. There is one easy way to tell the Floral reproductions. Take off the top and look at the threads where the lid

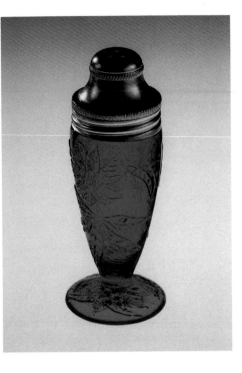

screws onto the shaker. On the old there are a PAIR of parallel threads on each side or at least a pair on one side which end right before the mold seams down each side. The new Floral has *one continuous line* thread which starts on one side and continues around the shaker until it ends above the beginning line on the other side. There is approximately one inch of overlapped thread making two lines for that inch; but the whole thread is *one continuous line* and not two separate ones as on the old. No other Floral reproductions have been made as of May 1992.

NEW "FLORENTINE NO. 1"
IMPORTING COMPANY OUT OF GEORGIA

Although a picture of a reproduction shaker is not shown, I would like for you to know of its existence.

Florentine No. 1 shakers have been reproduced in pink, red, and cobalt blue. There may be other colors to follow. I only have one reproduction sample, and it is difficult to know if all shakers will be as badly molded as this one. I can say by looking at this one shaker that there is little or no design on the bottom. No red or cobalt blue Florentine No. 1 shakers have ever been found so those are no problem. The pink is more difficult. I am comparing this one to several old pairs from my shop. The old shakers have a major open flower on each side. There is a top circle on this blossom with three smaller circles down each side. The seven circles form the outside of the blossom. The new blossom looks more like a strawberry with no circles forming the outside of the blossom. This repro blossom looks like a poor drawing! Do not use the Floral thread test for the Florentine No. 1 shakers however. It won't work for Florentine although these are made by the same importing company out of Georgia.

NEW "MADRID"
(amber, pink, crystal, blue, teal)
FEDERAL GLASS COMPANY, 1976–1977, 1980s, 1990s

Introduced by Federal as "Recollection" in 1976 ostensibly for the Bicentennial. Each piece is dated '76 as shown here on a plate edge. The color is a deeper amber than the old.

The butter dish knob has mold marks running from north to south on the new; the mold marks run east to west on the old. I mention this only because on occasion new tops are "married" to old bottoms in an attempt to do a bit of "wool pulling."

Other items introduced in 1977 are candleholders, creamer and sugar with no lid, a footed candy and cover, a footed square bowl and a footed cake plate. These last three footed pieces are not duplicates of the original Madrid. However, due to the first issues not selling so well, many stores failed to stock these latter pieces.

Indiana Glass is at it again. They continue to issue glass in colors made originally. Instead of creating new collectibles in colors never made, they insist on wiping out many a collector's dreams of financial profit by remaking glassware long discontinued. Shown at the top on page 145 is the "new" Recollection Pink Madrid. Thankfully, not much pink was made in the 1930s when Federal made Madrid. The picture at the top shows new concepts in design that were never made. There are other pedestal pieces using the candlestick for the base besides the cake plate shown. Once you have seen the pale, washed-out pink on any of these items, you will never have trouble spotting these culprits.

The bottom picture shows glassware similar to that made in the 1930s but of those, only the oval vegetable and cup and saucer were made in pink by Federal. The original pink is deep like Sharon's pink. Although I omitted showing the candlesticks, the new ones have ridges inside the opening to grasp the candle while the older did not. I might add that the new candles have shown up in BLACK.

A special thanks to John and Trannie Davis for furnishing the "Recollection" for this book. The better department stores were the first to have these items, but the discount houses are now advertising them so you will see lots of this in pink, crystal and blue as time goes by.

Blue has been made in all of the pieces shown in pink. It is a vivid blue when compared to the older subtle shade "Madonna Blue" made by Federal originally. The newest color is teal, which is a very greenish shade of blue.

NEW "MAYFAIR"

(pink, green, blue, cobalt [shot glasses], 1977 onward; pink, green, "brownish" amethyst, cobalt blue, red [cookie jars], 1982; pink, red, cobalt blue [shakers], 1988...)

Mayfair cookie jars, at cursory glance, have a base of which has a very indistinct design. It will feel smooth to the touch, it's so faint. In the old cookie jars, there's a distinct pattern which feels like raised embossing to the touch. Next, turn the bottom upside-down. The new bottom is perfectly smooth. The old bottom contains a 1¾" mold circle rim that is raised enough to catch your fingernail in it. There are other distinctions as well; but that is the quickest way to tell old from new.

In the Mayfair cookie lid, the new design (parallel to the straight side of the lid) at the edge curves gracefully toward the center "V" shape (rather like bird wings in flight); in the old, that edge is flat, a straight line going into the "V" (like airplane wings sticking straight out from the side of the plane as you face it head-on.)

The green color of the cookie jar, as you can see from the picture, is not the pretty, yellow/green color of true green Mayfair. It also doesn't "glow" under black light as the old green does.

So, you see, none of these reproductions give us any trouble; they're all easily spotted by those of us now "in the know!"

The shot glass (which is hard to find in the original) has also been made in this pattern. The green (totally wrong shade) and blue are no problem since the shot glasses have never been found in these colors originally. The difficulty comes with the pink.

Generally speaking, the newer shot glass has a heavier overall look. The bottom area tends to have a thicker rim of glass. Often, the "pink" coloring isn't right; it may be too light, it may be too orange. However, if these cursory examinations fail, there are other points to check.

First, notice the stem of the flower. You have a single stem in the new flower. At the base of the stem in the old glass, the stem separates into an "A" shape. Further, look at the leaves on the stem. In the new design, the leaf itself is hollow with the veins molded in. In the old glass, the leaf portion is molded in and the veining is left hollow. In the center of the flower, the dots (anther) cluster entirely to one side of the old design and are rather distinct. Nothing like that occurs in the newer version.

Repro Mayfair Shaker

	Old	New
* Diameter of opening	¾"	⅝"
Diameter of lid	⅞"	¾"
Height	4¹⁄₁₆"	4"
Corner Ridges on Shaker	Rise ½ way to top then smooth out	Rise to top and are quite pronounced

* Most immediately noticeable factor.

Thanks to Millie and Bill Downey for the use of the blue Mayfair shakers.

NEW "MISS AMERICA"
(crystal, green, pink, ice blue, red amberina)
PRIVATELY PRODUCED 1977

The new butter dish in "Miss America" design is probably the best of the newer products; yet there are three distinct differences to be found between the original butter top and the newly-made one. Since the value of the butter dish lies in the top, it seems more profitable to examine it.

In the new butter dishes pictured, notice that the panels reaching the edge of the butter bottom tend to have a pronounced curving, skirt-like edge. In the original dish, there is much less curving at the edge of these panels.

Second, pick up the top of the new dish and feel up inside it. If the butter top knob is filled with glass so that it is convex (curved outward), the dish is new; the old knob area is concave (curved inward).

Finally, from the underside, look through the top toward the knob. In the original butter dish you would see a perfectly-formed multi-sided star; in the newer version, you see distorted rays with no visible points.

Shakers have been made in green, pink and crystal. The shakers will have new tops; but since some old shakers have been given new tops, that isn't conclusive at all. Unscrew the lid. Old shakers have a very neatly formed ridge of glass on which to screw the lid. It overlaps a little and has neatly rounded off ends. Old shakers stand 3⅜" tall without the lid. New ones stand 3¼" tall. Old shakers have almost a forefinder's depth inside (female finger) or a fraction shy of 2½". These vary as there are reproductions of the reproductions! New shakers have an inside depth of 2", about the second digit bend of a female's finger. (I'm doing finger depths since most of you will have those with you at the flea market, rather than a tape measure.) In men, the old shaker's depth covers my knuckle; the new shaker leaves my knuckle exposed. New shakers simply have more glass on the inside of the shaker – something you can spot from 12 feet away. The hobs are more rounded on the newer shaker, particularly near the stem and seams; in the old shaker these areas remained pointedly sharp!

New Miss America tumblers have ½" of glass in the bottom, have a smooth edge on the bottom of the glass with no mold rim and show only two distinct mold marks on the sides of the glass. Old tumblers have only ¼" of glass in the bottom, have a distinct mold line rimming the bottom of the tumbler and have four distinct mold marks up the sides of the tumbler. The new green tumbler doesn't "glow" under black light as did the old.

New Miss America pitchers are all perfectly smooth rimmed at the top edge above the handle. All old pitchers that I have seen have a "hump" in the top rim of the glass above the handle area, rather like a camel's hump. The very bottom diamonds next to the foot in the new pitchers "squash" into elongated diamonds. In the old pitchers, these get noticeably smaller, but they retain their diamond shape. Only the non-ice lip pitcher has been reproduced!

151

NEW "SANDWICH"
(crystal)
ANCHOR HOCKING GLASS COMPANY

At present, only the cookie jar has been re-introduced to use the jargon of today. However, we may assume that if sales are good for this item, we may see others. The newer jar is much larger when compared with the old. To date, no other pieces have been made (May, 1992)!

	New	Old
Height	10¼"	9¼"
Opening Width	5½"	4⅞"
Diameter/Largest Part	22"	19"

NEW "SANDWICH"
(amber, blue, red, green)
INDIANA GLASS COMPANY, Tiara Exclusive Line 1969 . . .

In recent years, Indiana Sandwich in amber, the smokey blue shown here, and a sprayed red over crystal have been issued. In 1969 came red in quite a few pieces and these are difficult to tell from the older pieces of the 1930s. Any piece you see in amber or blue is of recent origin.

Bad news for collectors came in 1978 when Tiara announced that they were going to issue the Sandwich in crystal from decanter sets down to the domed butter dish. My advice here is to be wary of paying any high prices for the old at this time. Since many of the original molds are being used, there is little difference.

Green is now being made but it is a pale, washed-out green and will not glow under a black light as does the original green.

NEW "SHARON"
(blue, dark green, light green, pink, burnt umber)
PRIVATELY PRODUCED 1976...

A blue Sharon butter turned up in 1976 and created a sensation. The blue was the color of Mayfair blue; but this color was unknown in Sharon pattern. This fluke helped to quickly inform Depression enthusiasts that new editions were being made available.

In similar colors, you can distinguish between the old and the new butter dishes by noticing that the bottom ridge of the newer butter dish is sharply defined; the old bottom ledge is barely defined. Also, the top of the newer butter dish is heavier and thicker than the old – in most instances, it even weighs more. The knob is easier to grasp on the new butter dishes as it sticks up higher and you've more room to fit your finger around the knob and grasp the top. In the old butter dish. tops, the knob fits so closely to the top that it makes it hard to grasp the knob.

In 1977 a "cheese dish" appeared having the same top as the butter. I put the name in quotes because it is but a parody of the original cheese dish. The new bottom of the dish is about half-way between a flat plate and butter dish bottom and is over thick, giving it an awkward appearance. The real cheese dish bottom more nearly resembles a salad plate with a raised rim. These "cheese dishes" are easily spotted as being new.

The newest reproduction in Sharon is a too light pink creamer and sugar with lid. They are pictured with their "Made in Taiwan" label. These sell for around $15.00 for the pair and are also easy to spot as reproductions. I'll just mention the most obvious differences. Turn the creamer so you are looking directly at the spout. In the old creamer the mold line runs dead center of that spout; in the new, the mold line runs decidedly to the left of center spout.

On the sugar, the leaves and roses are "off" but not enough to DESCRIBE it to new collectors. Therefore, look at the center design, both sides, at the stars located at the very bottom of the motif. A thin leaf stem should run directly from that center star upward on BOTH sides. In this new sugar, the stem only runs from one; it stops way short of the star on one side. OR look inside the sugar bowl at where the handle attaches to the bottom of the bowl. In the new bowl, this attachment looks like a perfect circle; in the old, its an upside-down "v"-shaped tear drop.

As for the sugar lid, the knob of the new lid is perfectly smooth as you grasp its edges. The old knob has a mold seam running mid circumference. You could tell these two lids apart blind-folded.

While there is a hair's difference between the height, mouth opening diameter, and inside depth of the old Sharon shakers and those newly produced, I won't attempt to upset you with those 16th and 32nd of a degree of difference. Suffice it to say that in physical shape, they are very close. However, as concern design, they're miles apart. The old shakers have true-appearing roses. The flowers really LOOK like roses. On the new shakers, they look like poorly drawn circles with wobbly concentric rings. The leaves are not as clearly defined on the new shakers as the old. However, forgetting all that, in the old shakers, the first design you see below the lid is a ROSE BUD. It's angled like a rocket shooting off into outer space with three leaves at the base of the bud (where the rocket fuel would burn out). In the new shakers, this "bud" has become four paddles of a windmill. It's the difference between this 🦋 and this 🦋.

The shakers wholesale for around $6.50 a pair.

A Sharon candy dish has been made by the infamous St. Louis group. It is very crude, thick and should pose no problems. Be aware that it does exist and *know your dealer.*

Glossary of Terms

Amber - brownish yellow color (see Madrid or Patrician photo for example).

Amethyst - a light, pastel purple as opposed to black amethyst which appears black until held to strong light whereby it shows deep purple.

Apricot - a dark yellow color, yet lighter in shade than amber; usually used to describe the darkest shade of Princess than topaz.

AOP - abbreviation for "all over pattern," usually used to describe Cherry Blossom.

Berry Bowl - term used by many glass companies to describe a round bowl.

Bonbon - a candy dish, usually uncovered.

Bread and Butter Plate - usually a 6" plate in a pattern that does not have a sherbet.

Cake Plate - a heavy, flat plate, usually having three legs.

Carnival - older, iridized glassware from early 1900s; also term used to describe the color of Floragold or an iridized pattern.

Celery - usually a long, narrow, flat dish; in Colonial, a two-handled dish taller than the sugar.

Cheese Dish - a covered dish, the bottom of which is normally flatter than that of the butter dish. .

Chigger Bite - a term auctioneers use to describe a small chip on a dish.

Chop Plate - a large, flat plate called a salver by some companies.

Chunked - a polite way to describe a badly damaged piece of glass.

Claret - tall goblet of varying size depending upon company terminology.

Closed Handled - having solid tab handles.

Coaster - glass liner sometimes doubling as an ashtray.

Cobalt Blue - a deep, dark blue color (shown in Moderntone or Moondrops).

Comport/Compote - term used to denote small, open candy dish which is stemmed.

Concentric Rings - circles within circles; gradually increasing or decreasing sized circles.

Console Bowl - centerpiece bowl, usually with candlesticks.

Cordial - small goblet of varying size depending upon company terminology.

Cracker Jar - term for what would a modern-day cookie jar; they were sold with certain brands of products packed inside them.

Cream Soup - a two-handled bouillon or consomme dish.

Decanter - usually a stoppered bottle for wine.

Delphite - a light blue opaque color; sometimes referred to as "blue milk glass."

Demitasse - a smaller than normal cup with saucer.

Domino Tray - a tray with a ring for creamer to reside in; the remaining surface within the tray being meant to hold sugar cubes.

Ebony - black color.

Etched - design cut into glass; usually found on better quality glass.

Fired-On - color applied and baked on at the factory.

Flashed-On - color added over crystal; usually wears off as opposed to the fired-on color which does not wear off with use.

Flat - a non-footed dish; dish without a footed base or stem.

Fluted - scalloped edge.

Frog - heavy glass holed flower stem holder.

Goblet - a stemmed, bowl-shaped tumbler.

Gravy Boat - oval-shaped bowl used for serving gravy; often with a type of spout.

Grill Plate - a usually tri-sectioned plate of the type used in restaurants to keep the meat and vegetables divided from each other.

Hat Shaped - bowl looking like an up-turned hat.

Hot Plate - glass plate used for setting hot items on the table as a protection for the table or table spread.

Ice Blue - very light, crystal blue color.

Ice Bucket - a milk bucket-like container for holding ice cubes.

Ice Lip - a guard or fold molded about the lip of a pitcher to keep ice from falling out into the glass when pouring from the picther.

Jadite - an opaque, light green color.

Jam Jar - small, covered jar for holding jam or preserves.

Luncheon Plate - usually an 8" or 9" plate, smaller than a dinner plate.

Mayonnaise - an open, cone-shaped compote or flat with underliner.

Milk Glass - a white glassware, the color of milk, usually heavy.

Mold/Mould - a usually two-part encasement into which hot glass is poured and a glass object is formed; depression glass was primarily a glassware made from molds rather than being blown or formed by hand.

Monax - white color produced by MacBeth Evans, usually very thin.

Motif - the pattern or design on glass.

Mug - a heavy cup, usually flat bottomed.

Nappy - old word denoting a bowl.

Opalescent - white rimmed flowing into color.

Open Handled - handles having an opening for the finger or hand to reach through.

Parfait - a tall, ice cream dish of the type used for sundaes in soda fountains.

Pickle Dish - an oblong dish used for serving pickles; smaller than a celery.

Platinum Band - an applied silver colored rim on glassware.

Platonite - Hazel Atlas heat-resistant white glass often colored by a fired-on process.

Platter - oblong or oval-shaped meat dish.

Preserve Dish - tall, footed dish often used as a candy.

Rayed - arrows or spoke-like designs on glass bottoms.

Relish - oblong dish, sometimes referred to as a pickle dish.

Rolled Edge - glassware having an edge curved in toward or out away from center.

Rope Edge - glassware with and edge having a rope-like design embedded in it.

Rose Bowl - small, curved-in edged bowl, usually having a small center hole and usually tri-footed.

Salad Plate - usually 7"-7½" plate, for serving salads.

Salver - large, 11"-12" non-handled serving plate.

Sandwich Server - a salver or sometimes a handled, often center-handled, serving plate.

SASE - short for self-addressed, stamped envelope.

Sherbet - small, usually footed, ice cream or dessert dish.

Teal - a blue-green color by all companies except Jeannette.

Tidbit - a two- or three-tiered serving dish made of increasingly smaller plates connected by a center metal pole, around 12"-15" tall.

Topaz - bright yellow colored glassware.

Trivet - a three-footed hot plate, usually about 7" in diameter, similar in design to three-footed cake plates but much smaller in diameter.

Tumbler - a glass.

Tumble-Up - a glass bottle with long neck having a small tumbler seated upside-down over the bottle neck serving as the bottle top; usually used on nightstand by bed.

Ultra-Marine - Jeannette's blue-green color.

Vaseline - a glowing yellow colored glassware similar to the color of the jell-like substance of the same name.

A publication I recommend:

DEPRESSION GLASS DAZE

THE ORIGINAL NATIONAL DEPRESSION GLASS NEWSPAPER

Depression Glass Daze, the Original, National monthly newspaper dedicated to the buying, selling and collecting of colored glassware of the 20's and 30's. We average 48 pages each month, filled with feature articles by top-notch columnists, reader "finds," club happenings, show news, a china corner, a current listing of new glass issues to beware of and a multitude of ads!! You can find it in the DAZE! Keep up with what's happening in the dee gee world with a subscription to the DAZE. Buy, sell or trade from the convenience of your easy chair. **One Year Subscription - $19.00.**

Name _____

Address _____

City _____ State _____ Zip _____

Foreign subscribers - please add $1.00 per year

☐ Check Enclosed   ☐ Please Bill Me   ☐ MasterCard   ☐ Visa

Card Number _____ Exp. Date _____

Signature _____

Send to: D.G.D., Box 57GF, Otisville, MI 48463.
(Please allow 30 days.)

Additional Books by Gene Florence

Collectible Glassware from the 40's, 50's & 60's	$19.95
Collector's Encyclopedia of Akro Agate Glassware, Revised Edition	$14.95
Collector's Encyclopedia of Depression Glass, 10th Edition	$19.95
Collector's Encyclopedia of Occupied Japan I	$14.95
Collector's Encyclopedia of Occupied Japan II	$14.95
Collector's Encyclopedia of Occupied Japan III	$14.95
Collector's Encyclopedia of Occupied Japan IV	$14.95
Collector's Encyclopedia of Occupied Japan V	$14.95
Elegant Glassware of the Depression Era, 5th Edition	$19.95
Florence's Standard Baseball Card Price Guide, 5th Edition	$ 9.95
Kitchen Glassware of the Depression Years, Revised 4th Edition	$19.95
Very Rare Glassware of the Depression Years	$24.95
Very Rare Glassware of the Depression Years, Second Series	$24.95
Very Rare Glassware of the Depression Years, Third Series	$24.95

Add $2.00 postage for each book ordered.

Copies of these books may be ordered from:

Gene Florence – P.O. Box 22186, Lexington, KY 40522
or
Collector Books – P.O. Box 3009, Paducah, KY 42003-3009

Schroeder's Antiques Price Guide

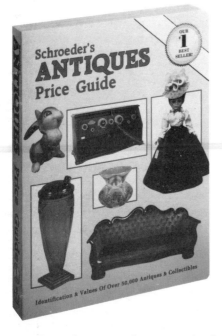

Schroeder's Antiques Price Guide has become THE household name in the antiques and collectibles field. Our team of editors work year around with more than 200 contributors to bring you our #1 best-selling book on antiques and collectibles.

With more than 50,000 items identified and priced, *Schroeder's* is a must for the collector and dealer alike. If it merits the interest of today's collector, you'll find it in *Schroeder's*. Each subject is represented with histories and background information. In addition, hundreds of sharp original photos are used each year to illustrate not only the rare and unusual, but the everyday "fun-type" collectibles as well – not postage stamp pictures, but large close-up shots that show important details clearly.

Our editors compile a new book each year. Never do we merely change prices. Each category is thoroughly checked to spot inconsistencies, listings that may not be entirely reflective of actual market dealings, and lines too vague to be of merit. Only the best of the lot remains for publication. You'll find *Schroeder's Antiques Price Guide* the one to buy for factual information and quality.

8½x11", 608 Pages   **$12.95**

COLLECTOR BOOKS

A Division of Schroeder Publishing Co., Inc.